MORE BEAUTIFUL YOU

A Study of True Beauty

Based on the #1 hit song
"More Beautiful You"

by Jonny Diaz

with Gwendolyn Mitchell Diaz

Harrison House
Tulsa, OK

The author has emphasized some words in Scripture quotations in italicized type.

13 12 11 10   7 6 5 4 3 2

More Beautiful You
ISBN 10: 1-60683-027-9
ISBN 13: 978-1-60683-027-7
Copyright © 2010 by Gwendolyn Mitchell Diaz, Jonny Diaz
205 Lewisburg Ave.
Franklin, TN 37064

What Others Are Saying

"'More Beautiful You' is one of those special songs that transcends music and has a real effect on people's lives."

— The Joy FM

"Hey! I am a 13-year-old girl, and your song, 'More Beautiful You', has impacted me in such a way . . . I feel that God placed me at the right spot at the right time. Every day I am tempted with people and society telling me what is right, how to dress, how to act. For a while, I felt like there was no hope for our society. Then I heard your song. Thank you, GOD."

—Nikki

"jonny, when i was 14 i thought i would be beautiful only if i lost just a little weight. well, i started losing weight and didn't stop. i kept thinking just 5 more pounds. i ended up anorexic. i'm 16 now and i'm not really anorexic anymore, but i still struggle with thinking that i'm not good enough. i heard your song more beautiful you and it really made me think that i'm always beautiful to god and he loves me the way i am. thank you so much for writing that song."

—Anonymous

"I just love your song 'More Beautiful You.' I can relate to that song from when I was a 14-year-old girl. I, too, felt that way and that was 25 years ago. I now have a 12-year-old, and I try to tell her every day how beautiful she is, and she shouldn't let ANYONE tell her differently. I just know that your song will reach a lot of young girls and show them that what they see in or on the cover of a magazine is not what they should go by."

—Mary

"I was going through some tough things for a while, and I have recently found God. I turned on my local Christian radio station and I heard your song and I immediately started crying. I am fourteen, and I have been struggling with a lot of internal and external problems. You song has had a HUGE influence on my life…Thank you!"

—MC

Contents

Preface

By Jonny Diaz

"God doesn't call the equipped; He equips the called." More Beautiful You is proof this isn't just some cliché saying to stencil on the wall of a church youth room. Instead, it is an exciting reality we see scattered throughout Bible stories and modern-day miracles. Let's face it, a 26-year-old guy, who grew up with three brothers and no sisters, writing a song that has impacted the hearts of thousands of women . . . Now that's a miracle!

Every season is a season of change when you're a new Christian artist like myself. However, one thing has always been certain during my short musical career. Summer is the season for camps. As much as I enjoy the large crowds, tour busses, and the huge production that comes with opening for some of Christian music's most popular acts, nothing compares to the relationships I get to build during the few summer camps I play each year. It provides an entire week where late-night bus rides are replaced by late-night campfires, catering with the band is replaced by cafeteria food eaten with students, and autograph lines are replaced by honest (and sometimes deep) conversations. A typical three-hour concert night allows the audience a small glimpse into my life, but camps allow me a deep look into the lives of those in attendance.

I started writing "More Beautiful You" simply because I saw a need for it. At every camp I played, no matter what age group, I noticed a huge desire of the female students to feel beautiful. At first, I viewed this desire as a fault. I thought, *Surely if you want to feel beautiful, you're more concerned with yourself than God.* But as my burden for these girls began to grow, I started to realize this was a God-given characteristic. I started to see that the desire to feel beautiful isn't wrong at all. The fault comes when we start caring more about our culture's definition of beauty than God's. "More Beautiful You" was written to speak truth into the lives of those girls.

Within about an hour of writing, I had the first verse and the chorus of the song. At that point, I made one of the few truly wise decisions I've ever made. I asked for help! It wasn't that writer's block was keeping me from finishing the song. It wasn't that I thought the material I had was weak and in need of help. On the contrary, I quickly saw "More Beautiful You" had the potential to be a great song. As I moved forward, I thought it would be so much more impactful if I had the help of a female. Kate York, a fellow Nashville songwriter, helped me craft the remainder of a song that would not only impact my life but impact the lives of thousands of women around the world.

The first radio release from a new artist is always a tough uphill battle. But in the spring of 2009 we began to see "More Beautiful You" was really starting to connect with listeners. By the summer, it had become one of the most requested songs on the air. That fall it became one of the most-played songs on all of Christian radio. With the song's success came new touring opportunities, radio interviews, and thousands of new fans browsing my Facebook™ and Twitter™ pages. I was prepared for all of those things. However, nothing could have prepared me for the letters and e-mails I started to receive. Females of all ages began pouring their hearts out to me. I read of countless struggles with eating disorders, cutting, sexual impurities, past rape experiences, and even attempted suicides. These girls (feeling like they had nowhere else to turn) were turning to me for answers I simply wasn't prepared to give.

That's where this Bible study comes into play. I wanted to be able to answer those letters and e-mails with something more than, "I'll pray for you." I wanted to create a resource for young women to dive deeper into the issue of self-image. I wanted to create a study where you could see how the message of "More Beautiful You" is not just my opinion, but God's too. Whether you're the young lady who has attempted to take her life, or you're the girl who simply has never quite been at peace with who she sees in the mirror, this book is designed to take a deeper look into why God created you like He did.

It would have been foolish for me to try and write this Bible study myself. First, I'm much better at writing lyrics than I am at producing reading material. Second, I could never speak from experience. It's no secret that guys (although we have many other issues) don't face the same kind of physical pressures girls are bombarded with from TV, magazines, and (unfortunately) the lyrics to most pop songs. Therefore, I reached out to the most qualified person I know—my mom! She is a great writer, loves the Lord, loves people, has a HUGE knowledge of Scripture, and (most importantly) she's a woman. Although she's certainly not immune to the pressures our society places on women, she has been such a great example of seeing herself (and others) through a godly perspective. I pray this study will help you do the same. Now, it's time I get out of the way and truly make this a "girls' study." I leave you in her *very* competent hands.

Introduction

Remember when your mom used to call you in from the backyard for dinner, and you would scramble to get in your seat at the kitchen table before your brother or sister could snatch all the chicken nuggets? Her command, "Go wash your hands and face before you sit down, young lady!" seemed like such an unnecessary addition to the eating process.

Bath time was usually a fun time—but that was because of the splashing, bubbles, and jillions of toys you could line up along the rim of the tub.

Your reaction to having to brush your teeth before hopping into bed totally depended on what flavor of toothpaste your mom had purchased at the drugstore and whether or not she had remembered to put new batteries in your Princess toothbrush.

Back in those days, a few seconds with a bar of soap and a tube of toothpaste could prepare you for just about anything the day had to offer.

But I have a hunch that things have changed. No longer is your mom pushing you into the bathroom to get yourself ready for school. More than likely she's trying to drag you out of it so your little brother doesn't have to pee in the bushes before the car pool arrives.

That's because you have decided that how you look matters. It matters to your friends. It matters to your enemies. It matters to strangers, and most of all it matters to you.

Please, don't get me wrong. Nowhere in this study are Jonny and I going to assume cleanliness and appearance don't matter. They matter very much—even to God. (Maybe we should make that "especially to God"!)

But here's the problem: chances are God isn't even on the list of people you are thinking about when you are plucking your eyebrows, shaving your legs, or trying on a skirt in a dressing room at the mall. And the truth is He should be the first One you think about.

In this study, we will investigate the faulty images of beauty our culture is asking us to accept; we will look at the unique and wonderful beauty God has already given each one of us, and we will reflect on our own images in the mirror of His Word.

Jonny and I are praying that through this study you will grasp how beautiful you really are and that you will use the beauty God has given you to attract a distorted, discontent, and dingy world to Him.

With Love and Joy,
Gwen Diaz

Lyrics

More Beautiful You

Little girl fourteen flipping through a magazine
Says she wants to look that way
But her hair isn't straight her body isn't fake
And she's always felt overweight
Well little girl fourteen I wish that you could see
That beauty is within your heart
And you were made with such care
your skin your body and your hair
Are perfect just the way they are

There could never be a more beautiful you
Don't buy the lies disguises and hoops they
make you jump through
You were made to fill a purpose that only you could do
So there could never be a more beautiful you

Little girl twenty-one the things that you've already done
Anything to get ahead
And you say you've got a man but he's got another plan

Only wants what you will do instead
Well little girl twenty-one
you never thought that this would come
You starve yourself to play the part
But I can promise you there's a Man whose love is true
And He'll treat you like the jewel you are

So turn around you're not too far
To back away be who you are
To change your path go another way
It's not too late you can be saved
If you feel depressed with past regrets
The shameful nights-"hope to forgets"
Can disappear they can all be washed away
By the One who's strong can right your wrongs
Can rid your fears dry all your tears
And change the way you look at this big world
He will take your dark distorted view
And with His light He will show you truth
And again you'll see through the eyes of a little girl

—Lyrics by Jonny Diaz with Kate York

Features

This study is designed to be equally beneficial if you are doing it on your own or with a group of your peers. Although it targets teenage girls, many older women after hearing Jonny's song have expressed a desire to restore the self-esteem that was robbed during their youth. We pray the lessons in this book will help women of all ages discover their true beauty and incredible worth.

Each lesson in this Bible study is based on a lyrical line from the song "More Beautiful You" and will contain:

- A narrative discussing the issue from both a cultural and biblical point of view
- A "Looking at God's Word" exercise
- A "Looking in the Mirror" exercise
- A verse to memorize
- A guide for talking to God
- Quotes from people whose lives has been touched by the song "More Beautiful You"

It is important for you to spend time reading the Bible passages and reflecting on them if you want to grow in your understanding of God's perspective on beauty. And it is essential for you to complete the exercises designed to help you apply the lesson to your life if you want to experience the peace and joy God intends you to have. In addition, we hope you will find the quotes from others helpful as they share the work God has begun in their hearts. Perhaps they will help you express what is in your heart.

May your life be changed as you reflect on your image in the mirror of God's Word.

"Little girl fourteen flipping through a magazine says she wants to look that way"

Lyrics from the song "More Beautiful You"

Lesson 1

The World's Version of Beauty

With the help of television, magazines, and the Internet, criteria for the latest "in" looks, fads, and fashions are circulated and updated faster than we can say, *Seventeen*. By the time we make it to the mall to purchase the latest fashion trend in footwear, it has already been placed on a clearance rack.

Acceptable standards for beauty and bling are constantly thrown in our faces. It is estimated girls ages 11 to 14 years old are exposed to more than five hundred advertisements every day. And thanks to plastic surgery and Photoshop™, the criteria for what is considered beautiful has now escaped all boundaries of reality. Most of the models have been nipped, tucked, enhanced, and airbrushed to an unattainable perfection.

According to my observations and calculations from the media, the ideal female is somewhere in the 14 to 23-year-old range. She wears a size-2 dress, stands 5'9" to 6' tall, and weighs less than 110 pounds. She has wide eyes, perfect skin, and long, thick, glossy hair. The only detail open to much diversity is her bra size. If she's a model in a magazine, she's probably not even large enough to wear one, but if she's a movie star, she is sporting at least a D-cup.

I recently read that in an effort to keep up with the distorted images girls are exposed to, 8 to 12-year-olds in this country spend more than $40 million a month on beauty products and teenage girls spend another $100 million.[1] And did you realize cosmetic surgery procedures performed on girls eighteen and younger have nearly doubled over the past decade?

With all the images and options available, can a teenager ever be satisfied with the way she looks? Perhaps a more pertinent question is, "Will her friends allow her to be?"

Looking at God's Word

Take a moment now and read Genesis 3:1-24. Then answer the following questions:

1. Look at verse six: What three things about the fruit from the forbidden tree made it attractive to Eve?_____

_____

_____

_____

_____

2. How does our culture use these same three lures to entice us to seek more than God has already given us?_____

_____

_____

_____

_____

_____

3. What should Eve have done to avoid being seduced by the serpent to sin?_____

_____

_____

_____

_____

Ever since that incident in the Garden of Eden, women have been lured by beauty. It was a beautiful snake holding a beautiful piece of fruit that convinced Eve to disobey God and mislead her husband, transforming her perfect world into a place of pain and suffering.

The deception began with her eyes. It wasn't until Eve took a long look at the attractive fruit Satan offered that she began to desire the one thing she didn't have.

We must learn to guard our eyes from things that would distract us. We cannot let them linger in places that will cause our hearts to long for what God never intended for us.

- If wandering through malls filled with fashion finery creates too much temptation for us to resist, then we must find other places to spend our time.

- If perusing through magazines causes us to lose our focus on God and put it on ourselves, then we should cancel our subscriptions.

- If television shows and commercials jeopardize our satisfaction, then we need to find more productive ways to spend our time.

We will be far more successful in avoiding discontentment if we learn to refocus our vision.

Looking in the Mirror

1. Ask yourself:

a. What does beauty mean to me?_____

_____

_____

b. What aspects of beauty do I desire the most?_____

_____

_____

_____

2. Memorize Psalm 119:36-37:
Turn my heart toward your statutes and not toward selfish gain.
Turn my eyes away from worthless things;
preserve my life according to your word.

3. To do:

a. Watch thirty minutes of one of your favorite TV shows with these specific questions in mind: What does this show convey about beauty? Where does it focus my attention?

_____

_____

_____

b. What are some ways you should be guarding your eyes?

_____

_____

_____

c. How can these verses help you view beauty differently than the world does? _____

_____

_____

_____

3. Talk to God: Tell Him your thoughts and feelings regarding beauty and the images you are exposed to. Ask Him to help you live out Psalms 119: 36-37 in your daily life. _____

_____

_____

_____

_____

So, what should we do if we don't happen to look exactly like a supermodel in a magazine or a pop star on TV or the beauty icon being showcased on the Internet? Well, we have a choice: we can spend a lot of money and energy trying to achieve the elusive ideal, or we can check out what God says about beauty. That's what we'll do in the next lesson.

What Others Are Saying

"Thank you from the bottom of my heart for this song, Jonny. I can't tell you what this song did for me—it literally changed the way I look at myself. I am fourteen, and I've always struggled with hating myself and how I look, because I don't look like those skinny, beautiful models in magazines. I know now that I can't compare myself to those people, because even they don't look like that in real life. This is the best song I've ever heard, and I've shared it with all my best friends, and they agree with me. THANK YOU THANK YOU THANK YOU!!!!"

—CrissiJean

"I completely chanced finding the song 'More Beautiful You.' THANK YOU!!!! Although I'm not Christian (I'm not really sure of anything yet. :S) I found the song so beautiful I was almost reduced to tears. (It takes a lot to make me cry.) It's about time people started realizing that magazine are hideous pieces of Photoshopped models that make us feel awful about ourselves! At 17-years-old I have been influenced many times by the power of media—changing the way I dress, eat, and act. Now I am much more comfortable in my own skin and love being the individual I am."

—Kate

"When I compare myself to people at my school or girls in magazines, I look in the mirror and HATE the girl staring back. Makes me wanna throw a rock at the reflection. But after listening to this, I realize it doesn't matter cos God loves me and thinks I'm not pretty, not gorgeous, but BEAUTIFUL. :] Brings a tear to my eye. :']"

— Anonymous

"Beauty is within your heart"
Lyrics from the song "More Beautiful You"

Lesson 2

God's Description of Beauty

Have you ever stopped to consider the fact all beauty originates from God? Everything that is attractive to us is a product of His creativity. He made it; He understands it; He likes it; He shares it with us; and He loves that we are attracted to it.

Every time we "oooh" and "ahhh" over a little kitten or stoop to examine the petals of a flower or snap a picture of a colorful sunset, we are admiring God's handiwork.

But not all of God's artistry is tangible or external. God's greatest display of creativity is concealed inside each of us (and I'm not talking about bones and blood vessels). Unfortunately we are often so focused on what we can see with our eyes or touch with our hands we ignore what is most valuable to Him—the hidden treasure that is in our hearts.

In 1 Peter 3:3-4 we are told, "Your beauty should not come from outward adornment, such as braided hair and the wearing of gold jewelry and fine clothes. Instead, it should be that of your inner self, the unfading beauty of a gentle and quiet spirit, which is of great worth in God's sight."

This verse does not suggest looking good is wrong. But it does point out that God places far more value on our inner beauty than He does on our external appearance. True beauty lies inside hearts that are filled with God's love and controlled by His Spirit. Inner character is far more important to Him than the outward beauty displayed in fashion magazines.

God places far more value on our inner beauty than He does on our external appearance.

Looking at God's Word

Take a moment now and look up the following verses, and beside each one describe the aspects of beauty that are important to God.

1. Proverbs 11:16,22_____

_____

_____

2. Proverbs 31:30_____

_____

_____

3. 1 Timothy 4:8_____

_____

_____

How would you compare what is important to God with what is important to our society?_____

_____

_____

_____

_____

Have you noticed that there are no descriptions of any women in the Bible? We are vaguely informed some of them were lovely to look at but never are any of their physical features described for us.

This seems kind of strange to me since God took such great pains to clarify every detail of the ark that Noah built—including the number of decks and the size of the windows. And He gave us all of the complex dimensions of the temple He asked Solomon to build, including a list of the materials, colors, shapes, and fragrances. Yet we are never given God's definition of an ideal woman's shape, size, color, or profile (or a man's for that matter).

Although there are specific standards for inner beauty that we are instructed to maintain, there are no particular criteria for outward beauty that we are commanded to achieve. God is obviously uninterested in having all of us look the same. He loves diversity. (Did you know there are approximately 20,000 species of butterflies in the world?)[2]

The question we need to ask ourselves is this: where do we place the emphasis when it comes to beauty? Do we spend more time fixing our hair than we do focusing on our hearts? Do we calculate our worth based on our outward appearance (like most of the people in our culture)? Or do we base our worth on our inner character (which is important to God)?

Remember, a perfect body never bought anyone peace during a difficult experience; it never produced wisdom in dealing with a complicated relationship; it never granted anyone a free pass through the gates of heaven.

We must include three basic steps in our beauty regimen if we want our lives to display the true beauty God has created inside each of us:

1. True beauty comes from spending time with God. All His beauty secrets are written for us in the Bible. If we want to discover them, we need to read it every day.

2. We need to spend time praying—sharing our fears with Him and allowing Him to place His peace in our lives.

3. We need to learn from other Christians who can help us develop godly priorities and grow in our faith.

Looking in the Mirror

1. Ask yourself:

a. How much time do I spend each day working on my outward appearance? (List the things you do.)_____

_____

_____

_____

_____

b. How much time do I spend each day working on my inward appearance? (List the things you do.)_____

_____

_____

_____

_____

c. Who is the most beautiful woman I know according to God's standards? What makes her so attractive?_____

_____

_____

_____

_____

_____

2. Memorize 1 Samuel 16:7: "The Lord does not look at the things man looks at. Man looks at the outward appearance, but the Lord looks at the heart."

a. What are some specific ways that God wants you to view beauty differently than the world does?_____

_____

_____

_____

b. What are some things you can start to do today to make yourself more beautiful in God's eyes?_____

_____

_____

_____

3. Talk to God: Tell Him how you would like Him to help you grow to be more beautiful on the inside._____

_____

_____

_____

God has created each of us perfectly. There is not a single feature that became a part of our lives without His knowledge. Let's discuss this more in the next lesson.

What Others Are Saying

"I am going to be attending a new school this year, and I was really worried about what they (the 'popular' kids) would think of me. I love God, but I know how cruel the world can be sometimes. When I heard your song on the radio, I thought, *Wow, I am beautiful and I can be whoever I want. It doesn't matter what they think of me. I am special and God created me to be me, not some computerized, perfect model.* Thanks for helping me with my fears and teaching me to just trust that God is in control now. Nothing they can do or say to me matters anymore."

—Anonymous

"I am not a young girl—actually, I am fifty-two. In December I was diagnosed with breast cancer and underwent a mastectomy with reconstruction surgery. February to June I went through chemo and lost all my hair. I have always taken care of myself and taken pride in my appearance so these transformations to my appearance have been very hard on me.

"The song, "More Beautiful You," reminds me though that Christ living within me is what's important and not my looks. Every time I hear this song on JOYFM I am blessed! Through this journey God has walked with me and taken care of me every step of the way. Thank you for blessing me with this song."

—PG

"you do not know how much this song has helped me; i've got physical disablities and hafta have lotsa surgeries which leave me surgical scars, some from when i was just a newborn and i've always felt ugly and scarred and unbeautiful. this song has helped me look through that and see God—how beautiful He made me to be, and i just want to say thank you, so very, very much."

—Jenny

"You were made with such care—
your skin, your body, and your hair
Are perfect just the way they are"
Lyrics from the song "More Beautiful You"

Lesson 3

God's Perfect Creation

Some people say God's creation of Adam was the pinnacle of His genius and artistry—that all the fish, birds, beasts, and flowers that came before him were just props for the main event.

But I tend to think the creation of man was just a rough draft for His greatest masterpiece of all—the introduction of woman! Believe it or not, you are part of God's magnum opus.

I know you don't always feel that way. More often than not, you consider yourself to be pretty ordinary and kind of uninteresting. Maybe you even think of yourself as flawed. I know because I struggle with the same kind of thoughts myself. Sometimes I wonder what God was thinking the day He put all the details of my body together. Why did He give me such a long, skinny neck and jillions of freckles? Did the melanin machine malfunction the day I was being formed? And why couldn't I have been given a good pair of eyes?

We all have feelings of inferiority when it comes to our perceptions of the containers God has created for us to live inside. And those perceptions often lead us to believe we aren't very valuable to Him.

Yet Psalm 139 explains each one of us was intimately and intricately crafted by God while we were still inside our mother's womb. The psalmist makes it clear this unique body is the only one that can perfectly handle the details of each day He has planned for us. The result is we are all awesomely and wonderfully made. And He wants us to know that "full well." (Psalms 139:14.)

Looking at God's Word

Take a moment now to read Psalm 139:1-16.

1. What do verses 1-4 say about God's knowledge of you?___

_____

_____

_____

_____

2. What do verses 5-12 say about God's protection of you?___

_____

_____

_____

3. What do verses 13-16 say about God's creation of you?___

_____

_____

_____

Now read Isaiah 64:8.

1. Think about a potter who is working with clay to make a vessel. How involved does the potter have to be in the process

of forming the clay? How involved is God in forming every detail of your body and life?_____

_____

_____

_____

These verses explain we are very important to God. He knows every thought we think, every word we say, and every action we perform. He protects every movement we make. And every single day of our lives was written down in His "day planner" before we were even born.

But not only are we very important to God, we are also very beautiful. He purposely planned and precisely created every intricate detail of our beings. That means nothing about our physical design is a mistake.

When we do not accept the fact we are beautiful, we are insisting God is not a very good artist or He is a sloppy creator or He sometimes makes mistakes or He really isn't as involved in the process as the Bible says He is (which would make Him a liar).

The problem is we have been conditioned to judge beauty according to the same standards the world uses—the ones we see in magazines, at the movies, or on the Internet. But the truth is the world's standards are completely distorted.

True beauty, as seen through God's eyes, has nothing to do with the number that comes up on the scale, what size bra we wear, how pouty our lips are, or the way we look in a pair of designer jeans. True beauty becomes evident when we happily accept the attributes He has so precisely crafted into us and strive to use the abilities He has so generously gifted us with to bring Him glory and share His love in this world.

We have been conditioned to judge beauty according to the same standards the world uses. But the truth is the world's standards are completely distorted.

Looking in the Mirror

1. Take some time to literally look into a mirror.

a. What are some of the physical characteristics God designed for you that make you very special and unique?_____

_____

_____

_____

_____

b. What are some of the abilities God has given you that prove you are His masterpiece?_____

_____

_____

_____

_____

c. What are some of the characteristics inside your heart that make God very proud of you?_____

_____

_____

_____

_____

_____

2. Memorize Psalm 45:11:

The king is enthralled by your beauty;
honor him, for he is your lord.

a. Since God thinks you are beautiful, what is one way you can honor Him?_____

_____

_____

_____

3. Talk to God: Ask Him to help you see yourself the way He does._____

_____

_____

_____

So, why is it so hard to accept this? Why are we so incredibly concerned with how we look on the outside? In the next chapter we'll take a look at how the world tricks us into believing God made us so inadequately.

What Others Are Saying

"This song is a great reminder that God made each of us exactly how we are supposed to be whether that's a size 2 or a size 14. Beauty isn't measured in what size you are, but it's measured by your heart, and this song conveys that perfectly. So I would like to thank you with my whole heart for expressing the correct belief that every girl is beautiful no matter what size they are or what color their hair is, if it's curly or straight."

—Emma

"I am an 18-year-old girl from GA. I just listened to your song and God spoke to me through it. My favorite lines are, 'So there could never be a more beautiful you' and 'And you were made with such care your skin your body and your hair / Are perfect just the way they are.'

"These words mean so much to me as I have been recovering from anorexia this past year. It has been a long and hard journey, but God has taught me so much through it and He has been there every step of the way . . . This song drowns out the lies I believe to be true. It replaces the voices in my head telling me to just lose more weight and gives me hope that I just might be beautiful the way I am."

—Zakevia

"I wanted to thank you so much for your absolutely amazing song "More Beautiful You." You'll never know how much of an impact it had on me. I'd been really bothered with my size and felt miserable. I was not at all happy with the way God made me and started to 'fix' the way I was made by eating much, much less. When I heard your song on the radio, I was feeling dirty, miserable, and physically sick. But when I listened to the awesome words of your song, I nearly cried. I felt so ashamed of being so vain and basically slapping God in the face by saying the way He made me wasn't good enough. I cannot thank you enough for your song. I am now slowly becoming more comfortable with myself and becoming to accept the girl God made me. Thank you so much!!!!!"

—Anonymous

"Don't buy the lies, disguises, and
hoops they make you jump through"
Lyrics from the song "More Beautiful You"

Lesson 4

The World's Deception

Can you remember back a few years ago to the carefree days—
the days when so many of the things that concern and consume
you right now didn't matter at all?

- It didn't matter if your hair was a mess. Your ponytail
whipped back and forth as you sped around the cul-de-sac on
your brother's bike.

- It didn't matter how many calories an ice cream cone added
to your daily consumption. It was the best reward you could
possibly receive for completing all your chores.

- It didn't matter if your only sundress was a hand-me-down
from an older cousin. The fact she had worn it three summers
before made it even more special.

But then something happened and everything changed. One day you looked in the mirror and began to compare yourself to an external standard of beauty you had never considered before.

This change might have been triggered when your grandmother made an off-hand comment about the weight you had gained since she last visited. Or it could have been initiated when you and your friends decided the unrealistically thin model wearing an outlandishly revealing outfit on the cover of a fashion magazine looked super cool. Or it could have been the result of an unflattering nickname.

Regardless of how it happened, at some point society's lies snuck their way into your mind, and you began using its warped criteria to judge your beauty and evaluate your worth. You were left feeling imperfect and inadequate. And Satan started smiling.

He likes it when we base our worth and value on our external appearance. He wants us to believe outer beauty is one of the highest ideals we can seek. He is happy when we concentrate on fixing our "flaws" instead of using what God has given us to serve Him.

As a culture we are willing to do just about anything to make ourselves feel more beautiful. Enhancing external beauty has become one of the biggest industries in our country. Every year teenagers spend more than 20 billion dollars on products to make them feel better about their appearance.[3] We are obsessed with beauty.

Back when Jesus was here on earth, the Pharisees had elevated wealth to a status higher than true godliness. They worshiped money in much the same way our culture worships beauty. Listen to what Jesus said to the religious leaders about this idol they created: "You are the ones who justify yourselves in the eyes of men, but God knows your hearts. What is highly valued among men is detestable in God's sight" (Luke 16:15).

The distorted, airbrushed, collagen-enhanced, regimen-requiring beauty that is so highly valued by our society is robbing God of the time and effort we should be spending serving and worshiping Him. I am certain He finds it detestable. Beauty is not just an ideal in our culture any more—it has become an idol.

Every year teenagers spend more than 20 billion dollars on products to make them feel better about their appearance.

Looking at God's Word

Read the following Scriptures and answer the questions:

1. Exodus 20:22-23; 1 John 5:21:

a. What does God say about idols?_____

_____

_____

_____

_____

b. How can beauty become an idol?_____

_____

_____

_____

_____

2. Jonah 2:8-9:

a. What happens to people who cling to idols?_____

_____

_____

_____

_____

_____

3. Mark 12:30:

a. How can we avoid getting trapped into worshiping the idol of beauty?_____

_____

_____

_____

_____

b. What practical things can you do to apply this verse to your life?_____

_____

_____

_____

_____

When we apply our culture's standards, nobody is perfect. We all have weaknesses that can be exploited—weaknesses that make us vulnerable to the "solutions" that are so convincingly presented.

But here's the amazing thing—in 2 Corinthians Paul tells us it is through our weaknesses God can best reveal His strength. In chapter twelve, he tells us about a weakness he is struggling with. We are not told exactly what that weakness is, but we can apply the principle to our lives. In verses 8 and 9 Paul says,

"Three times I pleaded with the Lord to take it away from me. But he said to me, 'My grace is sufficient for you, for my power is made perfect in weakness.'" Then Paul adds, "Therefore I will boast all the more gladly about my weaknesses, so that Christ's power may rest on me."

God wants to use the very things that hurt us most to bring the greatest good into our lives. He wants to demonstrate His power in us—if we will let Him.[4]

During his time on earth, Jesus was always hanging out with hurting people. He offered ordinary, weak, and wounded people eternal life. Yes, He healed them physically, but His goal always was to make them spiritually whole.

Ever since Eve sinned in the Garden of Eden, God has been in the business of transforming weaknesses into strengths. The whole Bible is a history lesson of God taking people with flaws, replacing their weaknesses with His strength, and then using them to accomplish amazing things. Are you willing to let God replace your physical "weaknesses" with His beauty?

Looking in the Mirror

1. According to the lies taught to us by our culture:

a. What are some of your physical "weaknesses"?_____

_____

_____

_____

_____

_____

b. What are some of your strengths?_____

_____

_____

_____

_____

_____

2. According to Romans 12:1-2, what does God want you to do with your physical weaknesses as well as your strengths?_____

_____

_____

_____

_____

_____

3. Memorize Psalm 27:4

One thing I ask of the Lord,
this is what I seek:
that I may dwell in the house of the Lord
all the days of my life,
to gaze upon the *beauty of the Lord*
and to seek him in his temple.

a. Like the Psalmist David, what should your one desire be? What does he mean by the phrase, "that I may dwell in the house of the Lord all the days of my life"?_____

_____

_____

_____

b. What does he mean to "gaze upon the beauty of the Lord"?

_____

_____

_____

4. Talk to God: Tell Him some of the lies society wants you to believe about yourself. Ask Him to help you stop focusing on your flaws and start concentrating on Him._____

_____

_____

_____

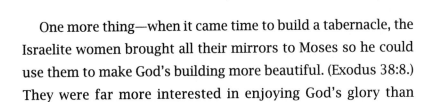

One more thing—when it came time to build a tabernacle, the Israelite women brought all their mirrors to Moses so he could use them to make God's building more beautiful. (Exodus 38:8.) They were far more interested in enjoying God's glory than reflecting on their own images.

Instead of searching for what the world calls beautiful, we should look at the One who created beauty in the first place. We need to get to know Him. Then we will fall in love with Him and want to serve Him.

We need to worship God instead of what this culture says is beautiful. His beauty never changes. It never fades. The more time we spend with Him, the more we will be transformed and His beauty will be seen in us. If we are going to be obsessed with anything, it needs to be God!

Once we put our focus on God rather than ourselves, our lives will be able to fulfill the specific purpose He has for our lives.

Instead of searching for what the world calls beautiful, we should look at the One who created beauty in the first place.

What Others Are Saying

"i've struggled with self image stuff since as long as i can remember. I have done quite a few things to try and change the way I look and make myself more 'beautiful.' when i heard this song on K-love it really touched me. the lyrics that say 'there can never be a more beautiful you, don't buy the lies disguises and hoops they make you jump through, you were made to fill a purpose that ONLY YOU can do' specifically spoke to me. thank you for allowing God to use you to share this amazing message."

—Aria

"i just felt i had to let you know how wonderful your song "more beautiful you" is, but i wanted to add that although there is such a strong desire women have to be beautiful and loved, it doesn't end at 21, trust me. women in their 30s and 40s are doing so much plastic surgery. i have a friend who is 31 last week tell me that she had decided to do Botox because she knew so many women younger than her getting it. i am not condemning any of this necessarily, i am just pointing out that i'm sure many women in their 70s would still love to be thought of as beautiful! and women of ALL ages struggle with a security about their appearance."

—Lisa

"You were made to fill a purpose
that only you could do"
Lyrics from the song "More Beautiful You"

Lesson 5

God's Perfect Plan

There is a story in the book of Acts that starts this way, "Now a man crippled from birth was being carried to the temple gate called Beautiful, where he was put every day to beg from those going into the temple courts" (Acts 3:2).

How ironic is that? A man, who was anything but beautiful by human standards, was dropped off at a gate called Beautiful every day. The man's lower limbs were so deformed he could not even get to the gate by himself. He was carried there then left to beg for food and money.

What makes this setting even more ironic is because of his deformity, the crippled man could be carried *to* the gate, but he could not be carried *through* the gate into the temple area. Since he was considered unclean, he had to stay outside while thousands of Israelites participated in the festivities and fellowship that took place inside the temple courtyard. So there he sat—an undesirable outcast on the outside of a beautiful gate.

Although the man was disabled from birth and discarded by society, God had an amazing purpose for his life—one only he, with all his deformities and pain, could accomplish. Through the lame man's hardship, God was able to demonstrate His incredible power in an awesome and dynamic way.

One day, as Peter and John entered the temple area through that same gate, they heard the man begging for alms. They had no money to offer, but Peter stopped and locked eyes with the crippled man. Then he reached out. The man grasped his hand and Peter lifted him to his feet. Immediately the man was able to walk, and jump, and shout for joy.

Can you imagine the scene? As the man ran through the gate for the first time, priests must have paused in the middle of their prayers. Levites probably stared in unbelief as they looked up from their incense offerings. People surely started clapping as the man who had sat outside the gate for so many years now danced in the marble courtyard. The Bible tells us everyone was "filled with wonder and amazement" at what had taken place.[5]

Peter was then able to share the message of God's love and power with all the people who gathered there. Over five thousand men accepted Jesus as their Messiah that afternoon. The scene at that gate certainly was beautiful!

Looking at God's Word

Read Acts 3:1-10 (the passage we just talked about).

After reading it, take some time to reflect on each of the following key words or phrases found in the passage. After reflecting on the phrase, answer the questions beside each one:

1. "The temple gate called Beautiful" (v. 2): Picture the setting in the context of the story. How do you think the lame man felt when he was placed there? Does this feeling connect with your life in any way?_____

_____

_____

_____

_____

_____

2. "At the time of prayer" (v. 1): How do you think the lame man felt about prayer? How does this feeling connect with your life?

_____

_____

_____

_____

_____

3. "To beg" (v. 2): What do you think the lame man thought each day as he began this humbling task? Is there an aspect of your life that allows you to identify with the lame man?_____

_____

_____

_____

_____

4. "In the name of Jesus Christ of Nazareth, walk" (v. 6): What do you think the lame man thought when he heard these words? If Peter saw you right now, what words do you think God would have him say to you? Is there an area in your life that needs healing?_____

_____

_____

_____

5. "Filled with wonder and amazement" (v. 10): How did this miracle impact the world around the lame man? What do you think God might want to do through your hardships?_____

_____

_____

_____

_____

_____

There's another aspect of this story I don't want us to miss. Not only is it important for us to realize God can redeem our problems and use them for good in our lives, He also wants us to be willing to reach out to serve others who have needs.

I'm sure Peter was in a hurry just like everyone else that day. An important prayer time was starting in the temple, but he took time out of his busy life to look straight into the eyes of a destitute man and focus on *the man's* needs instead of worrying about his own. Peter could have been distracted by the beauty of the gate, the crowds of people passing through, or all the duties he had to fulfill that day, but he wasn't. He saw a lame man, and he reached out to help him.

Isaiah 58:11 is a wonderful verse that describes God's desire to give us fulfilling lives. It says:

> The Lord will guide you always;
> he will satisfy your needs in a sun-scorched land
> and will strengthen your frame.
> You will be like a well-watered garden,
> like a spring whose waters never fail.

Isn't that neat? While everyone else's lives are shriveling up from the heat and frustrations of everyday life, God wants us to bloom like a garden in the middle of springtime.

But if you turn to Isaiah 58 in your Bible, you will find this fabulous promise given in verse eleven is attached to some very specific conditions. The preceding verses tell us that God will fill and satisfy us *if* we provide shelter for the poor wanderer and clothing for the naked. He will give us strength *if* we do not turn away from those who are in need. He will guide us *if* we use our energy on behalf of the hungry and spend our time meeting the needs of the oppressed. (v. 7)

If we want to find real purpose and happiness in life, we need to focus on other people just as Peter did. When we take our minds off ourselves, we give God the opportunity to fulfill our needs and lead us to places far more pleasurable than we could ever imagine. First Corinthians 2:9 tells us we cannot even conceive of the things God has planned for us!

God designed us to enjoy life the most and function at our best, when we are looking out for other people. Jesus says in Matthew 23:11, "The greatest among you will be your servant." No matter what our calling is, we will find the greatest success and joy when we serve others.

If we want to find real purpose and happiness in life, we need to focus on other people.

Looking in the Mirror

1. Read Galatians 1:10.

a. In what ways do you try to "please men"?_____

_____

_____

_____

b. How would things in your life be different if you chose to be a "servant of Christ"?_____

_____

_____

_____

c. What is one specific thing you can (and will) do this week to serve someone other than yourself?_____

_____

_____

_____

2. Memorize Luke 6:38: "Give, and it will be given to you. A good measure, pressed down, shaken together and running over, will be poured into your lap. For with the measure you use, it will be measured to you."

a. What does God promise you in this verse?_____

_____

_____

_____

b. Does this have anything to do with beauty?_____

_____

3. Talk to God: Ask Him to show you how you can fulfill His purpose for your life this week. Ask Him to give you a specific context where you can serve Him._____

_____

_____

_____

Like the song says, God has a purpose for your life that only you can do. I don't know what that purpose is, but I can guarantee you it involves trusting Him and serving others. As you trust Him, God will do amazing things in you just as He did for the lame man. And as you serve other people, He will also do amazing things through you just as He did with Peter.

While the world's definition of beauty causes us to try to gain things for ourselves, God's definition of beauty always causes us to give ourselves away. We will talk more about this conflict in the next lesson.

What Others Are Saying

"[I received] Two more calls this week about the song. One from a mom whose teen girl was ready to take pills because of the taunting she got at school. She heard 'More Beautiful You' and realized God loved her and had a plan for her...WOW!

"Played the song this morning and got a call from a 15-year-old who is exhausted from trying to be 'perfect.' She heard the song this morning, and it touched her and made her feel better. I'm humbled that I get to do what I get to do!"

—Brian

"I just wanted to thank you so much for your song "More Beautiful You." As I listened to it as I was driving one day, I realized that the song mirrored my own life. I had lost who I was. I had given into the world's view of who I should be. I had abused my body trying to be 'perfect' which resulted in eight years of eating disorders. But, God has washed me, fixed my distorted vision, and repaired my doubt in who I am as a person. You are correct. He does have a plan for me that only I can fulfill!"

—Hannah

"Jonny, I'm sure you've heard this a million times, but...WOW! As some background, I'm 21 years old and nowhere NEAR a perfect body. Satan's been working in my life to make me forget who my Creator is and focus on the negative and put me in a very dark place in my life in the last year. A couple of weeks ago, I hit rock bottom; I felt the absolute lousiest I think I've ever felt in my life. I was driving home from work, throwing a small pity party for myself, when a large deer jumped out in front of my car; had I hit it, I would have totaled my car, and if I swerved to miss it, I would have landed, tires up, in the ditch. By the grace of God, I somehow managed to miss the animal and pulled over to the side of the road to calm myself down. Since music is my escape, I flipped on the radio, which I had left tuned to KLOVE and heard the first few chords of a song that, I believe, has touched the life of every girl who has ever felt down on herself. God spoke to me that night through your music, and I cannot thank you enough. I now truly believe God has a plan for me and made me to His likings."

—Melodye

"Anything to get ahead"
Lyrics from the song "More Beautiful You"

Lesson 6

Our Longing to Be Noticed

Less than 100 years from now you and I will not be here. For one reason or another, we will no longer be on this planet. And very few people will remember we even existed.

Kind of startling when you really stop to think about it, isn't it? The question quickly becomes, do the things that occupy most of my thoughts and the majority of the time I am here really matter? Am I focusing on things that have eternal significance, or am I wasting my life chasing useless ideals?

Our sinful culture has introduced a false set of standards for beauty most of us have adopted as our own. We believe if we can achieve these standards, we will be rewarded with popularity and prestige—two of our most-sought-after goals. Therefore, vast amounts of our time and effort are spent trying to perfect our appearances.

Let me give you just one example. Chinese women have been deceived into believing height is the key to success. Many teenage girls are now undergoing an extremely lengthy and painful procedure to add inches to their stature. During this risky surgery, their leg bones are sawed apart, and a metal apparatus of levers and rods is inserted to hold the bones apart until they regenerate. Several rounds of surgery are required to readjust the levers and lengthen the bones. Unfortunately the results are sometimes uneven, and additional surgery is required to equalize the lengths. The cost of this procedure is more than double the annual income of the average Chinese household.

Why do Chinese women do this to themselves? It's because their society has chosen to equate height with beauty and power, and the women have accepted that standard. Some Chinese companies actually have height requirements for hiring (e.g., the foreign ministry requires female diplomats to be at least five feet, three inches tall).

When you think about this new practice, it is far more mutilating than the old tradition of binding women's feet to make them smaller. Yet our society actively sought to eradicate that practice. We adamantly insisted it was outrageous and wrong. But if making feet smaller is wrong, is making breasts larger,

noses shapelier, or legs longer really any different? They are all extreme methods of trying to get ahead in society by accepting its standards for beauty.

And, on a much simpler scale, isn't spending excessive amounts of time and effort applying makeup and perfecting our hair another way of accepting the same type of standards these Chinese women are clinging to?

When we accept the world's standards and try to transform ourselves to fit its images, we are saying God's blueprint for our lives and our bodies is wrong. We are questioning His knowledge, His power, and mostly His love.

Never in the Bible did God expect anyone to serve Him with anything more than what He had already given them. He never said, "Take what I have given you, make it more acceptable, and then use it to serve Me." No! He said, "Give Me what you have, and watch Me use it to do amazing things."

If Gideon had insisted on fighting the Midianites with more than the 300 ragtag men God had supplied for him, he would have been relying on his own strategies and strength more than on God's. God could not have used him to miraculously defeat the whole Midianite army made up of at least 135,000 soldiers.[6] (You can read Gideon's story in Judges 6 and 7.)

If the widow of Zarephath had insisted she didn't have enough flour and oil when God asked her to bake a cake for Elijah, she would never have experienced the miracle that allowed her to feed her young son until the terrible drought that devastated her country was over. (You can read her story in 1 Kings 17.)

God has given us exactly what we have in order to accomplish exactly what He wants. And that includes our looks!

Never in the Bible did God expect anyone to serve Him with anything more than what He had already given them.

Looking at God's Word

Read the original story of David and Goliath found in 1 Samuel 17:1-50.

1. Why was the Israelite army so fearful?_____

_____

_____

_____

_____

2. List at least three ways David fell short of the standards necessary to defeat Goliath._____

_____

_____

_____

_____

_____

3. How had God prepared David for this event?_____

_____

_____

_____

_____

4. What do you think would have happened if David had accepted the equipment that King Saul offered him?_____

_____

_____

_____

_____

A friend of mine recently told me this story about an experience he and his wife had. They were out-of-town guests at a wedding in a small town in Texas. After the "you may kiss the bride" and the last grandmother was escorted out of the small country church, they got into their car to drive a mile or so to the community hall for the reception. They followed a line of cars out of the parking lot, past the church, through the countyside, and then turned right at the first intersection. About half a mile down the road the lead car did a U-turn. My friend realized none of the dozen or so cars in the line had a clue where the reception was being held. They were all heading in the wrong direction and didn't know it. Eventually they found the hall and enjoyed a wonderful celebration, but my friend was amazed at how easily he had been led in the wrong direction.

Jeremiah wrote about this in the Old Testament. He said,
My people have been lost sheep;
their shepherds have led them astray

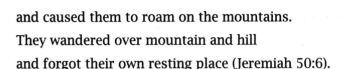

and caused them to roam on the mountains.

They wandered over mountain and hill

and forgot their own resting place (Jeremiah 50:6).

It is easy for us to lose our way when it comes to beauty by following the wrong people who have adopted the wrong standards.

Twenty-one times in the Gospels, Jesus told people to, "Follow me." If we follow Jesus, our primary goal in life will be to love God and love people just like He did.[7] Right now millions of Americans live in poverty not knowing where they'll get their next meal—yet we're upset if we don't have the right size hips, the right colored eyes, the right shade of blush, or the right . . . you name it. When it comes to the matters of life and beauty, the best way to avoid being led astray is to keep our eyes on Jesus and stay close to Him.

It is easy for us to lose our way when it comes to beauty by following the wrong people who have adopted the wrong standards.

Looking in the Mirror

1. Read Psalm 20:7.

a. When it came to battle, what did most people trust in? What did God want them to trust in? What does that mean—practically speaking?_____

_____

_____

_____

b. When it comes to beauty, what do people trust in? What does God want us to trust in? What does that mean—practically speaking?_____

_____

_____

_____

2. Memorize Zephaniah 3:17:

The Lord your God is with you,
he is mighty to save.
He will take great delight in you,
he will quiet you with his love,
he will rejoice over you with singing."

a. List five things that are mentioned in this verse that God wants to do for you._____

_____

_____

_____

b. How does God want you to apply this verse to your life right now?_____

_____

_____

_____

3. Talk to God: Ask Him to show you the false things you have been relying on to help you achieve popularity and prestige. Ask Him to replace them with the desire to trust Him—especially when it comes to what others think of you._____

_____

_____

_____

Our society tends to judge our value as women by the same standards it uses to judge livestock—our looks. But we don't need to accept society's standards in order to get ahead. As a matter of fact, we *cannot* accept them if we want to accomplish the purposes God has for us.

When we decide to follow God, we will not be focused on or upset by what we see in the mirror. When we choose to represent Him, His beauty will shine through us in ways that cannot be explained—and cannot be denied. People will see a difference in the way we look and dress. Hmmm—let's talk more about how we dress in the next lesson.

What Others Are Saying

"I know you've heard it over and over again, and so I'm sorry for this. I'm a college student who has struggled with my appearance my entire life, always questioning myself and putting myself down. I've been taken advantage of more times than I want to count by the men in my life, and my past is something I am always trying to run from and forget. Sometimes when I'm really feeling low and can't even look in a mirror, I listen to your song. And even if I can never believe it for myself 100%, I just wanted you to know that it helps."

—Lacey

"This is so true for me. I've tried starving myself for days on end trying to lose weight because I never felt thin enough. I used to cut myself because I never felt pretty enough. I would do things that I didn't want to because I wanted guys to like me. I wanted to feel loved. This song is just so perfect for me."

—Anonymous

"You say you've got a man
but he's got another plan"
Lyrics from the song "More Beautiful You"

Lesson 7

Our Longing to Be Loved

A lady I know who is a missionary in Africa wrote about the time her three-year-old daughter completely disrupted a village meeting when she walked in carrying a tiny chameleon. Immediately there was utter chaos as the adults clamored all over each other trying to get out of the room. They were absolutely panicked. Their eyes were wide with fear, and they ran from the room screaming.

Come to find out, these African villagers had been deceived into believing chameleons were filled with evil spirits. (How else would they be able to change colors and camouflage themselves so cleverly?) As long as that little girl held the reptile in her hands, the local residents would not come within ten yards of her. Once she realized she could manipulate them by taking advantage of their fear, that little girl had complete control over the entire room filled with adults.

One of the greatest fears a human heart can harbor is the fear of not being loved. Our culture is capitalizing on that fear and using it to manipulate our lives. In the last lesson we talked about how we have been deceived into believing beauty is a necessary precursor to power and prestige. Rather than trusting in God's plans for our lives and relying on His power to help us achieve His goals, we try to fit ourselves into a mold our culture has created. But the deception goes further. Society wants us to believe beauty is the primary requirement to find acceptance and love. And one of our greatest fears is not being loved.

Society wants us to believe beauty is the primary requirement to find acceptance and love.

This need for love is so important we are willing to compete for it. And the competition has become heated. We are willing to try to seduce anyone and everyone with the hopes someone might find us attractive and consequently fall in love with us. And as the bar for beauty continually rises, the criterion for decency seems to plummet. It is to the point some manufacturers are now specializing in the production of sexy lingerie for pre-teens.

Dressing seductively is wrong at any age. God designed men to be stimulated by what they see. (Women, on the other hand, are stimulated by what they feel both physically and emotionally.) In the book, *For Young Women Only* (Multnomah Books, 2006), Shaunti Feldhahn and Lisa Rice give the results of a survey in which guys are asked questions concerning the way girls dress. Eighty-five percent of the guys who took part in the study admitted when girls dress in a way that calls attention to their bodies, they are tempted to picture them naked (either then or later on).[8] The survey also showed the guys thought the girls were doing this on purpose.[9] But in a side-by-side survey only four percent of the girls acknowledged when they dressed in skimpy clothing, this is what they had in mind.[10]

For a girl to dress provocatively is wrong. Short shorts or skirts and low-cut or tight-fitting tops are lures that can lead a guy's mind down sinful paths. In 1 Corinthians 10:31-32, God tells us whatever we do, we must do it all for the glory of God. He adds this command, "Do not cause anyone to stumble." When we dress to attract attention to our bodies, we are dressing in a way that brings glory to ourselves instead of to God and, whether we want to or not, we are setting the scene to cause someone else to stumble. Both of these are sins!

Let me ask you a couple of questions: *If you catch a guy's attention by dressing provocatively, what are you telling him about yourself?* And, *if you were willing to use your body to entice him, what else are you willing to do with it in order to keep him?* Chances are the plans *he* has for your relationship are quite different from the ones you started out with. And one more thing: *What if he dumps you after you've given everything you have to try to keep him? How do you think it will affect you—spiritually and emotionally?*

Jerry Seinfeld once said, "Men don't care what's on TV. They care about what else is on TV." In other words—they get bored very easily and want to move on. Think about that in terms of a relationship that is based on physical attraction.

God makes it very clear in Scripture we are to remain sexually pure until we are married. He gave us this boundary in order to protect us from the deep wounds that can occur when a sexually active relationship suddenly falls apart. He knew that with each sexual encounter we give away a part of ourselves we can never get back—and we take away a piece of someone else we can never return.

Anything either partner in a relationship does to make the other partner desire to commit fornication (the biblical term for pre-marital sex) is sin. We need to remember this fact when we get dressed to go out with our friends.

Looking at God's Word

Read the following verses and answer the questions beside each one:

1. Ephesians 5:3: How does this verse apply to the methods many teenage girls use to attract teenage guys?_____

_____

_____

_____

_____

2. 1 Thessalonians 4:3–5: How should a Christian teenager look and act differently than one who does not have a relationship with God?_____

_____

_____

_____

3. 1 Corinthians 10:31–32: If you applied these verses to your life every time you changed your clothes, how would it affect your clothing choices?_____

_____

_____

_____

We talked about fear at the beginning of this lesson. The fear of not being loved is one of the most devastating emotions we can experience. Satan loves to cloud our judgment and convince us we need to change—we need to concentrate on fixing our "flaws" or lowering our standards in order to attract love. Fear causes us to do things we wouldn't ordinarily do or to participate in events we would ordinarily avoid. And, worst of all, fear keeps us from receiving many blessings God has ready for us.

There are so many good times God wants to share with us and so many great things He wants to give us, but when we react on the basis of our fears, we are unable to join Him. We can't reach out and accept what He is offering when our hands are occupied with fixing our "flaws" or clinging to someone God never intended for us to touch.

God created us with a space in our souls that can only be filled by Him. He intended for us to seek His love above everything else. No one else's love can fill that space. Do you remember what we said in lesson five? When we serve God, He promises to meet our needs and fulfill our desires. That includes the need to be appreciated and loved by a man. God knows exactly the right person who can fulfill our hopes, our dreams, and our needs.

I once heard a Christian teacher say, "Don't keep looking around for the right person to fall in love with. Run hard after God, and when you hear footsteps beside you, look over to see who is running along beside you. He will probably be the person God has chosen for you to spend the rest of your life with—the one who will fulfill your need for human companionship and love."

Until we conquer our fear of being solitary in a binary world, we will continue to be manipulated by society's deceit. We need to give that fear to God and trust Him to fill our lives with His unlimited and ultimate blessings.

God created us with a space in our souls that can only be filled by Him.

Looking in the Mirror

1.Look into your closet and drawers. Literally spend at least twenty minutes looking through the clothes and accessories and beauty products you own. Separate them into two categories:

a. Those that bring glory to God _____

_____

_____

_____

b. Those that bring glory to me _____

_____

_____

_____

Decide if there is anything God would like you to get rid of so He can fill your life with His blessings.

2. List your five greatest fears when it comes to life, love, and looks._____

_____

_____

_____

_____

_____

3. Memorize Psalm 34:4-5:

I sought the Lord, and he answered me;
he delivered me from all my fears.
Those who look to him are radiant;
their faces are never covered with shame."

4. Talk to God: Tell Him about your fears and ask Him to fill
you with His peace._____

_____

_____

_____

_____

_____

Our clothes reveal our hearts—whether we desire to bring
glory to God or draw attention to ourselves. But wearing modest,
God-pleasing clothing does not infer we should look out of
style or unattractive. Many women in the Scriptures dressed in
fine clothing and wore great jewelry. The ideal woman who is
so exalted in Proverbs 31 wore colorful, high-quality clothing.
(31:22.) Solomon's bride was adorned with beautiful jewelry.
(Song of Solomon 1:10-11.) And Esther underwent twelve months
of beauty treatments in preparation for seeing the King. (Esther
2:12.) Remember, God is the creator of beauty. He delights in it.

However, when we choose to dress in a way that exploits our sexuality, we choose a path that can very easily lead to destructive behaviors. Research shows three of the most common mental health problems diagnosed in girls start when they place an emphasis on their sexuality. These three are low self-esteem, depression, and eating disorders. We will talk more about them in the next lesson.

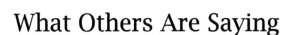

What Others Are Saying

"I am in my mid-twenties and just recently heard 'More Beautiful You' for the first time. Wow, it's amazing! I wish that song had been written when I was a teenager. After going from one abusive boyfriend to the next, I have always felt ugly until I got saved last year, and Christ changed the way I see myself. I will soon be speaking at a conference about domestic abuse and how God has brought me out of all that. There will be women from shelters and teenager girls there as well. I would really love to play your song 'More Beautiful You' for all of them to hear. Your music is such a blessing. I remember you and your ministry in my prayers."

—C. R.

"This guy has nonstop sexually harassed me through texting. I made friends with him, and I thought he was nice. Two years after we became friends, last year in other words, he started messaging me on Facebook™, telling me sexual stuff, and then it progressed to texting. He tried nonstop to get me to have sex with him, or phone sex, anything sexual . . . I heard this song, and about broke down into tears. This guy for a year now has made me feel like I don't deserve better. But this song made me realize I am better than that. That God can take me and make me new again. I will never be able to express how much this song has helped me. Every time I get depressed and scared and upset because of what this guy did to me, this song builds me back up.

So, thank you, from the bottom of my heart."

—Chelsea

"Hi Jonny! I love your song 'More Beautiful You.' I was driving home after work the other day and I heard it play on 89.3 KSBJ. I am 26 years old and for the past five years, I have been in such an abusive relationship (which I have gotten away from recently) that I couldn't see who I was anymore. My heart was battered in such a way that I could not even look in the mirror; I hated what I saw. In working through all of these emotions, this song is a constant reminder of just how God views me. It amazes me how His blessings come in such a small form but have such an intense effect! Like so many others, this song has truly been a blessing. Thank you so much!"

—Carrie

"You starve yourself to play the part"
Lyrics from the song "More Beautiful You"

Lesson 8

Our Longing for a Perfect Body

Have you ever read the book of Haggai? It's a tiny book in the Old Testament—just two chapters long. The events take place after the Jewish people are conquered by King Nebuchadnezzar and taken off as captives into Babylon. In the process, their land is devastated and their temple is destroyed. For seventy years they are not allowed to return to their country.

Haggai picks up the story as the Israelites return from exile and begin the process of rebuilding their country. They restore the city wall, erect fine houses for themselves, and finally, after a little nudging from God, they begin to reconstruct the temple.

However, as they work, the people become very discouraged. The temple they are working so hard to assemble looks nothing like the glorious temple Solomon had built almost 500 years before. It isn't large and expansive. It isn't filled with silver ornaments, and it doesn't glitter with gold furniture. In addition, they have to endure a lot of ridicule and harassment from the people who now occupy the land. The workers become so disheartened, they actually quit for a while.

So God speaks to them and makes this promise found in Haggai 2:7-9: "'I will fill this house with glory . . . The silver is mine and the gold is mine,' declares the Lord Almighty. 'The glory of this present house will be greater than the glory of the former house.'"

God informed them He owned all the gold and silver in the entire world. He could easily have helped them build another temple on the scale of Solomon's, but that was not His purpose. He wanted them to honor and obey Him with what He had given them instead of pouting because they wished they had more. He promised if they kept building, He would fill the new temple with a glory even greater than the old one that they were comparing it with. The glory would come, not from the building's outward appearance, but from God's presence. And that's just what happened. Jesus, himself, entered that smaller temple when He was here on earth!

In the New Testament, we are told our bodies are temples of God. No longer are we required to attend an external temple if

we want to meet with God. When we accept the sacrifice Jesus made for us on the cross (a concept we will talk more about in lesson ten), God's Spirit immediately comes to live inside each of us. Isn't that an incredible thought.

The glory would come, not from the building's outward appearance, but from God's presence.

Looking at God's Word

Read the following verses and answer the corresponding questions:

1. 1 Corinthians 3:16-17:

a. What does it mean to defile or destroy the temple of God?

_____

_____

_____

_____

b. What are some ways we do this in our culture?_____

_____

_____

_____

_____

2. 1 Corinthians 6:19-20:

a. Why are we not our own?_____

_____

_____

_____

_____

_____

b. How were we "bought at a price"?_____

_____

_____

_____

_____

c. What are some ways we can honor or bring glory to God with our bodies?_____

_____

_____

_____

_____

Can you see yourself and your attitudes reflected in the story recorded by Haggai? I certainly can! So easily and so often I get discouraged with how my temple looks. When I compare it to other temples, it seems to fall far short. It isn't the right size or shape. It isn't glitzy or glamorous enough. Sometimes other people ridicule it.

In a reverse situation from the Israelites, I get upset if my structure is bigger than the ones I choose to compare it to. I get all bent out of shape if I don't look like the thin models who walk the runway or pose for magazine ads. Instead of allowing my temple to be a place for God to live and work, I want to give up or go on a renovation rampage.

I know I'm not the only one who feels this way. The National Association of Anorexia Nervosa and Associated Disorders states that at least 8,000,000 people in the United States have eating disorders, and 90 percent of them are women.[11] I was shocked to discover how early this problem appears in our culture. According to a 2004 study by the Dove Real Beauty campaign, 42 percent of first to third grade girls want to be thinner, and 81 percent of 10 year olds are afraid of getting fat.[12]

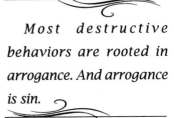

Most destructive behaviors are rooted in arrogance. And arrogance is sin.

Eating disorders cause great damage. They not only destroy our bodies, they consume our thoughts and emotions. Our bodies are holy places. For us to destroy or damage them in any way is just as bad as what King Nebuchadnezzar did to the temple Solomon built. (And, if you read the story in Daniel 4, you will discover God greatly punished King Nebuchadnezzar for the blatant arrogance that caused him to destroy the temple and build a kingdom that made him look great in everyone else's eyes.)

After a lot of research and thought, I have come to the conclusion that most destructive behaviors are rooted in arrogance. And arrogance is sin. Choosing to harm the bodies God intricately designed for us is a dramatic way of saying God's wisdom and skill are not good enough for us. Sometimes it is a distorted way of punishing Him for what He has allowed to take place in our lives.

Although it may be difficult to accept, injuring our bodies by starving them, cutting them, over feeding them, over-exercising them, or abusing them with drugs and alcohol is a way of focusing on ourselves—on *our* desires and *our* needs—instead of on God. It's a way of saying, "I can handle this myself," instead of giving God the right to help us and heal our disappointments and hurts, which brings Him joy and glory.

One time I shared this concept with a young lady who immediately challenged me by asking, "Why is everything always about God?"

"If you ask me," she continued, "God is pretty selfish. He is always wanting us to bring *Him* glory! What's wrong with *me* getting a little glory?" At that point I realized she totally misunderstood God's love.

God loves us more than any other person in the entire world ever could. And the one aspect of His character He wants us to grasp more than any other is how great that love is. His greatest glory comes from His relationship with us.

- When we are filled with joy, it brings Him glory.

- When we have peace in our hearts, it brings Him glory.

- When we are content with what life offers us, it brings Him glory.

From God's perspective, everything is really all about us. If this were not the case, He never would have sent His Son to die for us.

When we focus on God instead of ourselves, and when we give Him the right to work in and through us regardless of how we feel about ourselves, He fills our lives with all the things that bring true peace and happiness. He heals all the things that are broken.

Because it is so difficult to change directions once you have started down a destructive path, I would advise anyone who finds themselves even thinking about injurious behavior to seek help from a counselor. You need to talk to someone other than your friends who is experiencing the same emotions and is going through the same events you are. Seek out someone (like a parent, teacher, youth worker, or school counselor) who can help you take your eyes off yourself and look straight into God's eyes where you will find true love and joy.

Looking in the Mirror

1. Consider this: God wants you to bring Him glory.

a. How does it make you feel to realize God wants you to bring Him glory? (Does this bother you or excite you?) _____

_____

_____

b. Why?_____

_____

_____

_____

c. What is one way you think He wants you to bring Him glory right now?_____

_____

_____

_____

_____

2. Memorize Deuteronomy 7:7-8: "The Lord did not set his affection on you and choose you because you were more numerous than other peoples, for you were the fewest of all peoples. But it was because the Lord loved you."

a. This verse was written to the Israelites, but how does it apply to you?_____

_____

_____

3. Talk to God: Tell Him what your biggest struggle is right now. Ask Him to help you. Ask Him to use it to bring glory to Himself—and joy and peace to you._____

_____

_____

_____

Just as the priests and Levites were required to maintain the temple God lived in during Old Testament times, we need to maintain the temples He lives in now—our bodies! It is important to find and sustain a healthy weight, to observe good eating habits, to practice good grooming habits, and to incorporate healthy exercise into our schedules. But most importantly, we need to stop comparing ourselves with others around us. God could have given us any body in the world, but He chose the one, we have for a specific purpose. It's the one He wants to use to reflect His glory.

We need to quit looking at ourselves in our silver-lined mirrors and allow our images to be reflections of His love for us. We will talk more about this tremendous love in the next lesson.

What Others Are Saying

"I am currently a senior in high school and have been struggling with anorexia since fifth grade. The winter of my freshman year, I became deathly ill and was hospitalized. It was the two weeks in the hospital when I realized how close to death my eating disorder had brought me and that something had to change. 'Recovering' has been the most difficult struggle (both mentally and physically) of my life (the eighteen years so far) . . . .

"I first heard the song on K Love and was in the car and didn't catch all of the words. But when I got home, I looked it up, and as the You Tube™ music video was playing, the lyrics sank in, and I felt tears build up in my eyes. By the end of the song I was sobbing. I can't put words to what I felt. Only one who has gone through the pain can truly know what it's like to have an eating disorder weighing you down; however, your song comes closer than any I have ever heard.

"I believe that sometimes God works in lives indirectly. He has the power to turn our hardships into miracles, drawing us closer to Him in the process. It is certain that we will have trials and tribulations in life, and I have certainly had one of mine at a very young age; however, it is how we choose to overcome them that makes us stronger.

"I used to wonder why God let me slowly deteriorate through starvation and exercise addiction. But I have learned why: through the process of recovery, he has #1—brought me closer to Him and #2—put extraordinary people in my life.

"So many things are uncertain in life, however I know one thing is true: without the hand of God keeping me up, I would not be here today. I hope you know how important your song is and will continue to be to me and so many girls struggling with the hardships of life.

"And I truly don't know what else to say but thank you."

—MH

"I heard your song 'More Beautiful You' on the radio, and it meant so much to me. I've always been insecure about my looks and recently have been suffering from bulimia. Your song gives me hope. It made me realize that God made me for who I am. What I look like doesn't matter—it matters what I do with this life. I've begun to get help and all because of a song I heard on the radio. Thank you. Thank you so much. My fiancé says he owes you so much for probably saving my life."

—Shannon

"I just wanted you to know how important the message in your song 'More Beautiful You' is to this generation. I am the mother of

a beautiful sixteen-year-old girl who has suffered with anorexia for three years now. The recent statistics are that one in four teenage girls suffer from some type of eating disorder. These girls need to hear they are wholly loved by an awesome God who created them for His purpose. You have done a tremendous job in relaying that message through the lyrics of this song. I pray that you will be heard by all those hurting girls all over the world and that the Holy Spirit will work through you and the talent that He has gifted you with."

—Keri

"The first time I heard 'More Beautiful You' I cried. I do not cry when I hear songs, except when God uses it to speak to me in hard times. I have struggled with an eating disorder longer than I care to think about, and I've been getting help with it over two years now. God has taken me on an incredible journey and shown me I can do and be so much more than I ever expected of myself—physically, mentally, professionally, etc. 'More Beautiful You' came out at another milestone in my life. I've prayed that God will teach me to see my body they way He sees it (and love it) so that I can accomplish His purposes in my life. He's definitely working on that with me already. As hard and painful as it is and will be, I know the truth and that it will all be worth it."

—Whitney

"There's a Man whose love is true"
Lyrics from the song "More Beautiful You"

Lesson 9

Accepting God's Love

Do you ever wonder what love really is? Have you found yourself thinking about a certain guy 24/7 and wondering if he could be "the one"? Chances are you may have even taken a quiz in some magazine to help you determine whether you have been lucky enough to find true love.

In *Romeo and Juliet*, William Shakespeare wrote:

Love is a smoke made with the fume of sighs.
Being purged, a fire sparkling in lovers' eyes.
Being vex'd, a sea nourish'd with lovers' tears.
What is it else? A madness most discreet,
A choking gall and a preserving sweet.
(Makes me think he didn't really have a clue!)[13]

The lyrics of so many songs we listen to allude to the fact that love is all we need to make us happy. Many people spend their whole lives searching for "true" love. So, what is it? Instead of focusing on what other people say, let's look at what the Bible says.

According to 1 John 4:7-8, love and God are one and the same:

Dear friends, let us love one another, for love comes from God. Everyone who loves has been born of God and knows God. Whoever does not love does not know God, because God is love.

Love is one of God's defining characteristics. Everything God says and everything He does is an expression of love. So, if we really want to know what true love is, it would probably be best for us to look at what He says about it. Fortunately for us, one whole chapter in the Bible is dedicated to explaining love from God's point of view.

In 1 Corinthians 13, Paul holds love up in front of us as if he was holding a diamond, and he then describes all of its facets. Each of them reflects an aspect of God's character. In the first three verses He tells us true love involves much more than just words—it requires actions. But he explains those actions must be more than the simple exercise of our abilities or the superficial sacrifice of what we possess. They must come from a

heart that seeks to do what's best for the other people involved. Then in verses 4 through 7, he describes all of the gleaming characteristics that make up true love. It is far more than an emotion—it is characterized by a series of choices we must make.

Everything God says and everything He does is an expression of love.

Looking at God's Word

Read 1 Corinthians 13:4-7.

1. List all the facets of true love that are described in these verses._____

_____

_____

_____

2. Beside each one write a choice that must be made in order for this facet of love to shine._____

_____

_____

_____

3. How is true love different from the type of love most teenagers experience or expect?_____

_____

_____

_____

To quickly summarize, true love puts the needs of another person above its own desires. It always seeks the best for them regardless of the difficulty or inconvenience that might result.

God displayed true love to its fullest extent when He sent Jesus to this earth to die for us. John 3:16 says, "For God so

True love puts the needs of another person above its own desires.

loved the world that he gave his one and only Son, that whoever believes in him shall not perish but have eternal life." This was the ultimate, most heart felt sacrifice He could possibly make for us. It didn't just involve Jesus suffering horrendous persecution and being nailed to a cross. It involved Him taking our sins and being separated from God so we never have to face this dreadful experience.

While He lived here on the earth, Jesus perfectly demonstrated true love in every aspect of His daily life so we would have His example to follow. Then He humbly and willingly went to the cross for us. Let's read what God says about Jesus' demonstration of "true" love in Philippians 2:1-11 as it is translated for us in *The Message* Bible:

> If you've gotten anything at all out of following Christ, if his love has made any difference in your life, if being in a community of the Spirit means anything to you, if you have a heart, if you care— then do me a favor: Agree with each other, love each other, be deep-spirited friends. Don't push your way to the front; don't sweet-talk your way to the top. Put yourself aside, and help others get ahead. Don't be obsessed with getting your

own advantage. Forget yourselves long enough to lend a helping hand.

Think of yourselves the way Christ Jesus thought of himself. He had equal status with God but didn't think so much of himself that he had to cling to the advantages of that status no matter what. Not at all. When the time came, he set aside the privileges of deity and took on the status of a slave, became human! Having become human, he stayed human. It was an incredibly humbling process. He didn't claim special privileges. Instead, he lived a selfless, obedient life and then died a selfless, obedient death—and the worst kind of death at that—a crucifixion.

Because of that obedience, God lifted him high and honored him far beyond anyone or anything, ever, so that all created beings in heaven and on earth—even those long ago dead and buried—will bow in worship before this Jesus Christ, and call out in praise that he is the Master of all, to the glorious honor of God the Father.

Wow, what would our world be like if we all could express and experience this kind of love.

In order to do that, there are several hurdles we must overcome. First, there is an issue of faith. We need to trust that from His vantage point, God has a better view of our circumstances than we do. We need to believe, regardless of how we feel at the time, the decisions God makes for our lives are always made with our best interests at heart. He sees what lies ahead and sometimes He places roadblocks in our way to keep us from continuing on a path that would lead to great injury.

Have you ever seen a fugitive hunt on TV? I watched one that was going on live the other day. One of the first things the lawmen on the ground did was bring in a helicopter to give them a better perspective. Several officers had decided to take a shortcut and jump a fence, but the helicopter pilot could see there was an ambush set up on the other side, so he stopped them. No matter how counterproductive it may have seemed to the officers on the ground at the time, they listened to the helicopter pilot and headed in the opposite direction taking a much longer (and safer) route around the house in order to apprehend the criminal.

God has a better view of our circumstances than we do.

Well, God has the most comprehensive and accurate view of what is going on in our lives. And it's not limited to what is happening right now. He knows everything that has ever taken place in the past, and He knows everything that will ever place in the future. Therefore, He completely knows what is best for us. We need to willingly consent to His plans and His decisions.

I've discovered the times we have the most difficulty understanding and accepting God's love are the times when we don't feel loved by others. For some reason, we blame God for their rejection of us instead of trusting Him to do what's best. We tend to think, *God, if You loved me, You would make them love me too,* when He knows they are not reliable enough to love us properly. We can only experience true love when we trust the One who designed it.

Another huge issue we struggle with is the fact our culture seems to have confused love with lust. According to what we read in 1 Corinthians 13, love puts the happiness, health, and spiritual growth of the other person above its own desires. Therefore true love does not engage in any activity that could possibly harm someone or lead another person to sin.

Lust, however, is a different story. Lust looks after its own needs and desires and uses others to fulfill them. God did not create lust. It showed up in the Garden of Eden when sin entered the world. It is mankind's perversion of God's character. It is the opposite of true love. Look at a few of the differences:

LOVE	LUST
Builds others up for their good	*Uses others for personal gain*
Gives what it has to others	*Gets what it wants from others*
Is patient and understanding	*Is impatient and pushy*
Is satisfied by serving others	*Always demands more*
Anticipates the future	*Only cares about the present*

We must never mistake lust for love. It will only rob us of God's best for our lives.

One of our greatest problems occurs when we decide that we are responsible for finding love. Instead of allowing God to fill the space in our hearts that can only be satisfied by His love, we search for love on our own. We fail to realize earthly love does not always last. Only God's love never fails. It will never change. And the only way to find true love is to focus on Him and allow Him to bring it into our lives.

We must never mistake lust for love. It will only rob us of God's best for our lives.

Looking in the Mirror

1. Take a few minutes and think about true love, and then list at least ten character qualities you desire for the man you will someday marry. What are some things you can (and must) do to make sure you won't ever settle for anything less?_____

_____

_____

_____

_____

_____

2. Memorize Ephesians 3:17-19: "I pray that you, being rooted and established in love, may have power, together with all the saints, to grasp how wide and long and high and deep is the love of Christ, and to know this love that surpasses knowledge—that you may be filled to the measure of all the fullness of God."

a. In your own words, what was Paul praying for the people who lived in Ephesus?_____

_____

_____

_____

_____

b. List the key words that stand out to you in this prayer. What is important about each of these words?_____

_____

_____

_____

c. What does Paul mean when he says Christ's love "surpasses knowledge"?_____

_____

_____

3. Talk to God: Ask Him to help you begin to discover how big His love is for you. Ask Him to help you seek only love that is based on His definition of true love found in 1 Corinthians 13.

_____

_____

_____

_____

We have talked about the fact that God is the essence of true love and Jesus is our example. But did you know there is nothing we can do to diminish or control God's love? Regardless of what we do, despite whether or not we want Him to, no matter where we go, God is going to love us more than we can comprehend. We will talk about this more in the next lesson.

What Others Are Saying

"I was in an abusive relationship and have spent the past few years struggling with custody of my son and trying to rebuild my self esteem. During the last week I have heard the song 'More Beautiful You' by Jonny Diaz several times, and each time it brings me to tears. I love it that he brings emphasis to the fact that we were made to fill a purpose that only we can do. But my favorite verse is "I promise you there's a man that's true that will treat you as the jewel you are." It was as if God spoke it right to my heart, and I finally understood how much He loves me and that He wants me to love myself too.

—Susan

"i love your song more beautiful you...when i first listened to it i started crying...your song just touches my soul and some lil girl is opened up...and i just cant believe how true your lyrics are...idk how you could rite a song that describes every girls life and especially mine...i suffered from a mild depression at 13 and now im 15 and free from it all and i hope you continue writing such inspirational songs for all us little girls out there."

—R**

119

"It's not too late you can be saved"
Lyrics from the song "More Beautiful You"

Lesson 10

The Beauty of Redemption

George Bernard Shaw, a famous Irish playwright who lived about a hundred years ago, described his infatuation with beauty this way:

> I believe in Michelangelo, Velasquez, and Rembrandt; in the might of design, the mystery of color, the redemption of all things by Beauty everlasting, and the message of Art that has made these hands blessed. Amen. Amen.

Shaw equated beauty with redemption, perfection, and blessing. It became like a god to him—something that had the potential to fix everything that was wrong in his life. He counted on external beauty—the kind he could see with his eyes—to bring him purity and happiness rather than focusing on the condition of his heart.

As a whole, our society has the same goals and focus that Shaw did except we try to find our redemption in our own personal appearance rather than the beauty we see around us. It has become a god to us—an idol like we talked about in lesson four. And we have established standards to help us know how well we measure up. The problem is these standards keep changing.

This may come as a surprise, but "thin" has not always been "in." For centuries, women were not considered attractive unless they were shapely, soft, and round. All the models who posed for the great masters like Michelangelo and Leonardo da Vinci were full-figured. As a matter of fact, curves were an essential aspect of beauty throughout most of history. Just half a century ago Marilyn Monroe was considered the ultimate icon of beauty, but today she would have a difficult job landing a media job—except maybe as a plus-sized model on a shopping network. However, due to health issues that are now emerging and markets that are currently dwindling, it probably won't be long before the fashion industry changes it standards again and full-figures will be back in vogue.

As long as we strive to achieve these external standards of beauty, we will remain frustrated and disappointed. As soon as we feel we measure up in some area, we realize that we fall short in another. Yet we continue to struggle, totally unaware that our drive for purity and perfection and our infatuation with beauty originate from an emptiness deep inside our souls—one that only God can fill.

You see, true beauty is the result of a relationship with God. It can never be reached by transforming our appearances or achieving some kind of harmony with nature. God is the One who created us. He is the One who placed the desire for redemption, happiness, and beauty inside each of us. And He is the only One who can fulfill it. In the Bible, He explains the criteria that must be met in order for us to have this relationship. Unlike society's standards, His never change.

As long as we strive to achieve external standards of beauty, we will remain frustrated and disappointed.

Looking at God's Word

Read the following Scripture passages and fill in the blanks:

1. God's Position:

a. John 3:16: God _____ all of us.

b. Matthew 5:48: But God is _____.

2. My Condition:

a. Romans 3:23: I have _____.

b. Isaiah 59:2: Because of my sins, I am _____ from God.

c. Romans 6:23: Because of my sins, I must _____ (be spiritually separated from God forever).

3. God's Provision:

a. Romans 5:8: Because God loves me, He sent _____ to die in my place.

b. 2 Corinthians 5:21: Because Jesus took my sin, I have become _____.

4. My Decision:

a. John 3:16: I must _____ in order to have eternal life.

b. Romans 8:38-39: There is _____ that can separate me from God's love once I have accepted what Jesus did for me on the cross.

God is holy; He is righteous. Nothing unholy or unrighteous can enter His presence without contaminating it completely. The problem is we are all sinners. There is no way that we can measure up to His perfect holiness and righteousness. Therefore, we have no chance of ever making it into heaven. We are doomed to die—to be spiritually separated from God—for all of eternity.

But God loves us so much He sent His Son, Jesus, to die in our place. Although none of us could ever live the perfect life required, Jesus could—and He did. He lived his entire life on this planet without ever committing a single sin! He lived up to God's standard of holiness, and He offered His perfect life as a sacrifice for our sins.

Jesus didn't just experience physical death when He was crucified on the cross; He experienced spiritual death. He was spiritually separated from God. He was willing to experience the horror of hell so we will never have to. But in order for Jesus'

sacrifice to be credited to us, we must believe He really did this for us and accept His payment for our sins. We must thank Him for His amazing act of love and begin to live our lives based on His standards.

When we acknowledge our inability to get to heaven on our own and we accept Jesus' substitution for us, God no longer sees the sin that separated us from Him. When He looks at us, He sees Jesus' holiness instead. Then God declares we are righteous and worthy to be in His presence. And once we are there, nothing— absolutely *nothing*—in all of heaven and earth can separate us from Him ever again. How awesome is that?

Because of God's love and Jesus' sacrifice, we are holy, perfect, and beautiful. Yes, beautiful. Psalm 29:2 and 96:9 explain beauty, majesty, and splendor (depending on your translation) come from God's holiness—which we now share. True beauty can only come from a relationship with God. And with that pure beauty comes peace and happiness.

True beauty can only come from a relationship with God.

Looking in the Mirror

1. God created an emptiness inside each of us that can only be filled with His love. What things are you using to try to fill the hole in your heart right now? How are most of your friends trying to fill the holes in their lives?_____

_____

_____

_____

_____

_____

_____

_____

2. Memorize John 15:13: "Greater love has no one than this, that he lay down his life for his friends."

a. What are three things this verse tells you about Jesus' love for you? _____

_____

_____

_____

_____

_____

_____

3. Talk to God: Have you ever made the decision to accept Jesus' sacrifice on the cross?

a. If not, ask God to help you comprehend the tremendous sacrifice Jesus made for you. Ask Him to help you understand how only a relationship with Him can fill the longing in your heart. Let Him know you believe in Him—that He died for you and was raised back to life so He could have a relationship with you. _____

_____

_____

_____

_____

_____

b. If you have accepted Jesus, thank God for loving you enough to send Jesus to die in your place. Thank Him that nothing can ever separate you from that love. Thank Him that with that love comes a beauty that is filled with peace and happiness. Ask Him to let others see that beauty shining through your life. _____

_____

_____

_____

_____

_____

In our society, beauty has become a religion of its own with its own set of commandments that dictate what we should and should not wear, how much we should or should not weigh, where we should or should not go, and who we should or should not be seen with in order to be accepted as beautiful. We elevate celebrities to sainthood based on how quickly they get back in shape after having a baby, their lack of cellulite in a swimsuit, or how noticeable they are on a runway. We believe the cutoff for reaching heaven and happiness is a size two.

But society's standards are fickle, and external beauty quickly fades. I'm sure you can name many beautiful people whose beautiful lives fell apart over the past year leaving them in an unholy, unhappy mess. But the beauty, purity, and happiness that come from a relationship with God are permanent. They can never be taken away. In the next lesson we will talk about how we can practically experience God's beauty and love regardless of what may have taken place in our past.

What Others Are Saying

"I just turned twenty-one and I am a junior in college, and I am going through a lot of horrible things right now. I am feeling more shameful and guilty then I ever have before for things in my past. This song is amazing and says it all. God loves us no matter what we do and always lets us start new and sees us as beautiful."

—Anonymous

"I am a grandmother and age fifty-seven. The song 'More Beautiful You' came on my favorite Christian radio station yesterday, and it was the first time I had ever heard it. I just want you to know what it did for me. First I saw, in my mind my beautiful eight granddaughters ranging from 6 to 15 in age as I listened. They, too all try to be what society expects of them. It is sad to watch. They are so wholesome and beautiful right now, I can hardly describe them as I see them! I just watch them in AWE! All eight of them love the Lord and that alone makes them amazing. But, of course society makes them feel not quite enough. There are freckles on some; there are glasses on some; there are imperfect extremities on some. The imperfections are decided by society, of course. Hearing your song made me see each one of them for how they feel about themselves vs. how I actually view them. Amazingly, our Father sees them at an even greater amount of perfection than I do. So, I thank you for your song. They will each be getting a copy of it. By the way, I said I was fifty-seven at the start of this message. I told you that because you even ministered to me at this age about all the pain I have felt for most of my life knowing I was not beautiful by society's standards. Your song made me realize how beautiful I am by my Father's standards, and He is what counts! We win in the end of the story, don't we? God bless you for doing his work through the songs He has and will continue to put in you to minister for Him!!!"

—Linda

"Again you'll see through
the eyes of a little girl"
Lyrics from the song "More Beautiful You"

Lesson 11

The Beauty of Restoration

Do you know when we accept the sacrifice Jesus made for us on the cross, we become daughters of the King of the universe? John 1:12 says, "To all who received him, to those who believed in his name, he gave the right to become children of God."

How awesome is that? We are princesses! We are real-life characters in the greatest fairy tale ever told—except it's not a fairy tale—it's a true story. In the beginning, we were struggling little waifs trapped in a world filled with sin and suffering. But the King of the universe sent His only Son, a Prince named Jesus, to come and rescue us. The Prince loved us so much He was willing to sacrifice His life for us so one day we would be able to live in the castle with His Father. But the King used His awesome super powers to raise His Son from the dead, and now both of them are waiting for us to come join them in the castle ballroom for the greatest party ever planned.

As daughters of the King, not only are we going to live with Him in heaven in the future, but He allows us to have a fresh start while we are still living here on earth right now. Second Corinthians 5:17 says, "Therefore, if anyone is in Christ, he is a new creation; the old has gone, the new has come!"

Have you ever heard of a mulligan? In golf, it is the opportunity to re-take a shot—the first one doesn't count, and you get to do it over. Well, this is the ultimate "do over." All of our sins—past, present, and future—are forgiven when we accept the sacrifice Jesus made for us on the cross. Everything we have ever said or done wrong is erased. All of our bad choices are excused. When God looks at us, He no longer sees our sinfulness. Instead He sees Jesus' righteousness in its place. (We talked about this in lesson ten.)

The Bible is filled with examples of God rescuing people and giving them fresh starts in life before He took them to live with Him in Heaven.

- I can immediately think of Rahab, a Canaanite prostitute, who put her trust in the God of Israel. (You can read her story in Joshua 2:1-14 and 6:25.) Not only was she forgiven for her sins, she ended up joining the Israelite nation and becoming an ancestor of Jesus Christ. (Matthew 1:5.)

- And then there was David who slept with a beautiful lady named Bathsheba and then had her husband murdered. How awful was that? Yet, when he admitted his sin, God forgave him and used him to continue ruling the nation of Israel. (2 Samuel 11-12.)

- And let's not forget the apostle Paul who persecuted all the Christians he could get his hands on before Jesus appeared to him when he was on the road to Damascus. (Acts 9:1-6.) His life was completely transformed, and he became God's spokesman to the Gentile nations.

The Bible is filled with examples of God rescuing people and giving them fresh starts.

Looking at God's Word

1. Read Psalm 51.

a. According to the introduction written prior to verse 1:
Who wrote this psalm?_____
When did he write it?_____

b. What does David admit to God?_____

_____

_____

_____

_____

c. What does David ask God to do?_____

_____

_____

_____

d. Based on this Psalm, what are some things we should do
when we know there is sin in our lives?_____

_____

_____

_____

_____

2. Read Psalm 103:1-5 and list six benefits that accompany God's forgiveness._____

_____

_____

_____

_____

_____

Although Jesus' sacrifice paid the penalty for all our sins, in order to experience God's cleansing, we need to ask for His forgiveness just as David did. First John 1:9 says, "If we confess our sins, he is faithful and just and will forgive us our sins and purify us from all unrighteousness."

One of the problems we have is, as we continue living on this planet, the nice clean lives God has given us tend to start collecting clutter. You know what I'm talking about because the same thing happens after you've cleaned out your closet. For a while it's spotless, and you love it. You feel so relieved to be rid of the mess. But then you get rushed, and you leave your jeans hanging on the doorknob and your sweater on the floor. A few days later you can hardly open the door to find your shoes.

Our lives get cluttered in the same way, and God is the only one who can clean them up. But He is a gentleman. He doesn't barge in and fix things unless we invite Him. Just as David did,

we have to confess what we have done is wrong and ask for His forgiveness and cleansing.

We know sin can never affect our *relationship* with God once we are His daughters. (We saw this when we looked at Romans 8:38-39 in lesson 10.) But it can affect our fellowship with Him. It's just like your relationship with your parents. You will always and forever be their daughter. Nothing can change that fact regardless of what takes place in your life or either of theirs. What can change is your rapport with each other and how much you enjoy being around each other.

When we choose to disobey or ignore God's standards, our companionship with Him can become very strained, and His presence in our lives can grow quite awkward. When we sin, it is hard for us to look Him in the eyes. Instead of seeing His love, we begin to picture Him as imposing, mean, and eager to punish us. We may forget He is our heavenly Father and more than anything else, He wants to enjoy His relationship with us—so much that He sent His Son to die for us. The reason He wants us to live up to His standards is so we can enjoy all the benefits that belong to His children—the benefits David mentions in Psalm 103:2-5.

Did you notice in 1 John 1:9 and also in Psalm 103 that God doesn't want to just temporarily forgive us? He wants to purify or cleanse us. He wants to get rid of the root of the problems that cause us to sin. He wants to satisfy our desires with good things, not the bad things that always leave us hurting and hungry. And He doesn't want us to miss out on any of the enjoyment He planned for us, especially in our youth. He wants us to be able to look at life through the eyes of an innocent little girl. But the first thing we need to be able to do is to admit the truth—to tell God where we have messed up. And then we need to invite Him to clean up our lives.

Looking in the Mirror

1. Are there things in your life that are keeping you from enjoying a relationship with God?

a. If so, list them (very privately if you want to)._____

_____

_____

_____

_____

b. Share them with God, and ask Him to forgive you, cleanse you, and help you live an uncluttered, care free life. _____

_____

_____

_____

_____

c. Tell God about any unmet desires you have and ask Him to satisfy those desires with "good" things. (Psalm 103:5.)_____

_____

_____

_____

_____

_____

2. What is one way you wish you could see life through the eyes of a little girl again?_____

_____

_____

_____

_____

(Is there anything or anyone that has robbed you of enjoying your childhood? If so, talk to God about it. Then I would strongly encourage you to talk to an adult you can trust—like a youth leader, pastor, or school counselor. Sometimes we need someone else to help us deal with difficult issues from our pasts.)

3. Memorize Isaiah 43:18-19:

"Forget the former things; do not dwell on the past.
See, I am doing a new thing!"

4. Talk to God: Ask Him to clean the dirty things and fix the broken things from your past. Ask Him to help you forget the hurtful things and allow Him to do amazing new things in and through you. Ask Him to help you live life with the carefree joy of a little girl. _____

_____

_____

_____

Just as with any beauty regimen, the beauty God desires us to have begins with cleansing. When we experience His cleansing work in our lives and begin to use the products (the Scriptures, prayer, and fellowship with others who believe) He has provided to enhance our true beauty, the beauty that is inside us will begin to shine through. Once again we will display the innocent loveliness of a little girl who hasn't yet felt the sting of humiliation, the pain of rejection, or the shame of bad decisions; a little girl who knows she will be accepted just as she is when she runs to Jesus for protection and courage (Luke 18:16,17), a little girl whose joy is evident in her confident smile. And we will begin to share this wonderful experience with others. Let's talk more about that in lesson 12.

What Others Are Saying

"Hey, Jonny! Your music is absolutely amazing. I got into my friend's car the other day and she had your 'More Beautiful You' CD playing. The beat really caught up with me, but then I started listening to the lyrics . . . and when I did . . . WOW. I want to thank you. I had been drifting away from God and my faith . . . . but the lyrics and your music has indeed restored my faith like a child. I went out and bought a copy of your CD and haven't been able to stop playing it since. It's on repeat in my stereo now. You truly are a great lyricist and again, I thank you for restoring my faith! And may God bless you in all that you do!"

—LJ

"Jonny,

"Thank you so much for your music. The song 'More Beautiful You' has quite a different meaning for me than for many of the girls on this web page. I'm not the girl at 14, but I'm the girl at 21 (24 to be exact). I'm a single mother of 2 year old and 1 year old boys. The part in the bridge about God's erasing the shameful nights you hope to forget is truly the story of my life. And even after my huge mistakes, He's somehow managed to make me into even a more beautiful person than I was before.

"I now have a special purpose—I'm trying to start a non-profit daycare chain and a ministry for single moms. This song always brings me to tears because it reminds me that even I was made to fill a purpose, and that God has used my mistakes to make me into the only person that can fill that purpose. Again, thanks so much, and God bless you!"

—Jana

"There could never be a
more beautiful you"

Lyrics from the song "More Beautiful You"

Lesson 12

Becoming a Model

Have you ever wondered why the King of the universe sent His Son to rescue us—and then just left us living here on earth? What's up with that? Why didn't Prince Jesus pull up on a white horse, let us jump on the back, and then whisk us off to His castle in the sky? Instead we are left in the same place, surrounded by all the same people, struggling through many of the same circumstances we were in before He ever entered our lives!

Well, it's because God has a very important job for us to do. He wants us to help Him rescue as many people as possible—people who otherwise would not have a clue there is a King who loves them and a Prince who was willing to die for them.

Right before Jesus took off to return to His Father's castle, He gave us several duties. One of them was that we should love each other in the same way that He loved us. That's pretty intense. He wants us to be willing to give up everything, including our physical lives so other people can have spiritual life. (John 15:12,13.) The very last commandment He gave before He left was for us to go everywhere in the world and tell everyone we possibly can the message that they, too, can be sons and daughters of the King of the universe. (Matthew 28:18,19). Wow, what a huge assignment!

But God did not leave us here to complete this humongous task without His help. He has provided us with everything we need to accomplish it. Look at Psalm 103:4-5 (the same verses we studied in the last lesson). Verse four tells us our Father (the King) has given us crowns—exactly what you would expect a princess to wear—to identify us as His children. The two crowns that set us apart and make us beautiful are love and compassion. They demonstrate to everyone our lives touch that we are not like everyone else—we are daughters of the King.

According to verse five, not only does God give us the things we need to complete our tasks, He satisfies our desires as well. If you read the verse carefully, you will realize it doesn't say God gives us everything we crave. It actually says He satisfies our desires with good things. So often the things we think we want

are not good for us. (Can you really imagine being married to a superstar? It could get pretty lonely. You would never get to see your husband. Or, how about that pony you've wished for since you were six years old? Could you really afford to raise it in your backyard?) God knows what is best, and He only gives us things that have significant value.

Not only does He give us all the things we need to complete His assignment (plus a few extras), in the last part of Psalm 103:5, God promises to give us the strength to complete the task.

To sum it up, our job while we are left here on earth is to be models. We are to model a lifestyle that is so different from everyone else's in this world they cannot help but notice it. It is a lifestyle characterized by compassionate giving. It is a lifestyle that reflects and radiates God's beautiful love. It is a lifestyle that will attract others to Him.

Crowns of love and compassion set us apart and make us beautiful.

Looking at God's Word

Read Matthew 5:14–16.

1. What metaphor does Jesus use to explain the type of models we are supposed to be?_____

_____

_____

_____

_____

2. List at least four distinguishing facts about light that are evident from these verses. _____

_____

_____

_____

_____

3. According to verse sixteen:

a. What should people see when they look at us? (Describe some of the good deeds that should make us stand out.) _____

_____

_____

_____

_____

b. What should people do when they see us?_____

_____

_____

_____

_____

Jesus knew this modeling assignment would not always be easy. Not everyone thinks light is attractive. In John 3:19-20, He says some people prefer to live in the darkness because it hides their evil deeds. All of the false images of beauty we are exposed to come from people who reject the light offered by God's Word. They refuse to accept its truths.

Let me share with you a letter from Lydia, a model in New York City who has made it according to the standards our world has set for beauty. Listen to her heart as she shares part of her journey:

> When I began modeling, I had no idea that I would still be doing it today. I had no real "passion for fashion"; it was just a way to make money while I was in college. It was a hobby at best! Now six years later I'm living in New York, modeling full time, and my achievements in my career have far exceeded my wildest dreams. I'm no supermodel . . . far from it, but all in all it has been a successful run for someone like me.

Over the years modeling has become my identity. Quite reluctantly I accepted the title and all of the stereotypes that came with it. I adopted the "lifestyle" and even moved to the biggest fashion city in America to pursue it. Yet, shortly after moving here, I realized that the fashion industry wasn't "it" for me.

I've never been shy or doubtful of myself, even when I tackle new tasks—they are an adventure in my eyes. Yet, after most days of castings, shoots, and shows, I would come home feeling a little less like me. The way I felt about myself and the world around me was quickly changing. Every day I felt more cynical and less confident. Offers of bigger paychecks and more publicity left me with an increasing sense of guilt and greed. The next big gig was like a drug to me; if I landed it I was on a high for days, but after that I was always looking for the next "hit." At times I would even start bargaining with God, asking Him for the most selfish of things. How was I honoring Him or giving glory? After a self-induced "time-out" and a lot of prayer, I realized that it was time to reevaluate my goals.

During this soul-searching time I realized two things:

1) I'm more than a model; my identity is not based upon my career. 2) The relentless pursuit of perfection is a waste of time and energy. Yet, these are the two things

the high fashion industry demands of its models: your identity and perfection. Well, news flash: that's not gonna happen! I'm not going to lose more weight, I'm not going to compromise my morals, and I'm not going to lie about my age. (I'm 25 and loving it!)

At the end of the day I will not allow myself to be molded by society's ever-changing definition of beauty or success. My happiness is not determined by how many gigs I land or how much money I make. Fame and fortune are too easily lost, and I'm yearning for something more permanent. I want my life to be about humility and love, not pride and envy. God made me with a purpose in mind, and that's what I'm living for.

—Lydia

Outward beauty brought Lydia photo shoots with some of the greatest photographers in the world; it allowed her to strut down world-class runways wearing famous designers' clothing; it placed her photo on a billboard four stories high in the middle of Manhattan; it took her to amazing parties; but it didn't bring her fulfillment. Lydia is no longer modeling for the fashion industry or for herself. She is modeling love and compassion as Jesus instructed us. She is finding her peace and contentment by helping needy people who live in her community.

Looking in the Mirror

1. Evaluate your image:

a. There is a Zulu tribe in South Africa where the members greet each other with a phrase that means, "I see you." Isn't that great? Do you really "see" the other people your life comes in contact with, or are you too busy wondering how they see *you?*

_____

_____

_____

_____

b. What have you done recently to provide light in a dark place?

_____

_____

_____

_____

c. God has given us crowns of love and compassion. Are you wearing yours? If not, what kinds of crowns distinguish your life?

_____

_____

_____

_____

2. Memorize 1 John 4:11: "Dear friends, since God so loved us, we also ought to love one another."

a. How does this verse impact your life?_____

_____

_____

_____

_____

_____

3. Talk to God: Ask Him to help you focus on others and their needs more than you focus on yourself and your needs. Ask Him to show you someone specific He wants you to share His love with this week and how He would like you to do it. Ask Him to help you become one of His next top models of true beauty.

_____

_____

_____

_____

_____

It is hard to keep our eyes focused on things we can't see (like the crowns, castles, and the future glory God has promised) when we are bombarded with all the false promises that accompany all the counterfeit images our culture uses to portray beauty. Jesus

knew this would be the case. As a matter of fact, just before he left to go back to His castle in heaven, He said, "In this world you will have trouble. But take heart! I have overcome the world" (John 16:33).

He understands the difficulties that confront us in our culture. He knows every day we have to face struggles emotionally, physically, and spiritually—especially when it comes to beauty. But His love is stronger than anything we will ever encounter. We need to keep our focus on Him. He is coming back to get us! He will take us home to live in God's castle with Him. Meanwhile, we must share His love and compassion with everyone God leads into our lives. That is what true beauty is really all about.

What Others Are Saying

"I am just fascinated by this song you wrote, 'More Beautiful You.' I wish I'd heard it when I was struggling with my weight as a kid. But now I'm so glad I can share it with my clients. Music is what got me through so much of the painful times of not finding God in the right places, and I'm just in a grateful place. So I hope to help girls believe in themselves who haven't quite hit their teen years yet, and to share it with women in their twenties in college who could relate as well.

"I'm working on self-esteem with some girls at a local youth sports camp with the Salvation Army, and I'm going to be playing your song in my class Friday."

—Meredith

"I LOVE THIS SONG! I think every girl, old and young, should hear this song! I pray that we all remember that God created us to be special. We as women can be our own worst enemies. Ladies, we need to stick together and not demean or belittle one another. We are ALL beautiful!"

—Anonymous

References

[1]www.newsweek.com/2009/03/29/generation-diva.html
If you want to check it out, it is in the second paragraph, under the subtitle "New Methods, Old Message".

[2]North American Butterfly Association website (www.naba.org/qanda.html) 2010

[3]"Spa Kids" by Michele Orecklin, *Time Magazine*, Vol. 162, No. 3 July 21, 2003

[4]Romans 8:28

[5]Acts 3:10

[6]Judges 8:10

[7]Luke 10:27

[8]*For Young Women Only* by Shaunti Feldhahn and Lisa Rice, Multnomah Books, 2006, page 96

[9]*For Young Women Only* by Shaunti Feldhahn and Lisa Rice, Multnomah Books, 2006, page 106

[10]*For Young Men Only* by Jeff Feldhahn and Eric Rice, Multnomah Books, 2008, pages 136-137

[11]http://familydoctor.org/online/famdocen/home/ children/teens/eating/277.html

[12]www.newsweek.com/2008/02/16/say-cheese-and-now-say-airbrush.html

[13]SparkNotes Editors. "SparkNote on Romeo and Juliet." SparkNotes LLC. 2007 http://www.sparknotes.com/ shakespeare/romeojuliet/ (accessed May 6, 2010).

Gwen's Bio

Gwendolyn Mitchell Diaz is Jonny's mom. In addition to Jonny, she and her husband, Ed, have raised three older sons, all of whom are grown, married, and love the Lord. Ed and Gwen currently have seven grandchildren. Their house is often chaotic but always fun.

Gwen is the author of several books, including *The Adventures of Mighty Mom: Here She Comes to Save the Day . . . If Only She Can Find the Keys!* This humorous book details some of the crazy experiences she had raising four very active young men. In addition, she has written three books for teenagers that deal in a very down-to-earth way with the current biblical and spiritual questions teenagers face. They are titled:

· *Sticking Up for What I Believe: Answers to the Spiritual Questions Teenagers Ask*

· *Sticking Up for What Is Right: Answers to the Moral Dilemmas Teenagers Face*

· *Sticking Up for Who I Am: Answers to the Emotional Issues Teenagers Raise*

All three books have been recently updated and published by Xulon Press. They are being used in Christian schools and youth groups all over the world.

Gwen wrote a newspaper column for several years and continues to write regularly for other national publications. She is passionate about presenting Christianity to teenagers and young men and women in a way that will capture their interest, satisfy their curiosity, and communicate God's exciting truths. She is delighted to have this opportunity to share in Jonny's ministry by helping him write this very important study about true beauty.

For more information:

Go to Gwen's website at www.gwendiaz.com.

Jonny's Journey

When Jonny Diaz headed off to Florida State University on a baseball scholarship in the fall of 2002, he was prepared to focus his time and efforts on his athletic skills. However, God had other plans, and He began a work in Jonny's life that led him to put down his bat and glove and pick up his guitar instead. Jonny was the fourth of four brothers to attend college on a baseball scholarship, and two of his brothers have played ball at a professional level (Matt Diaz is currently the left fielder for the Atlanta Braves), so it's easy to understand the enormity of this decision. But, with God opening the doors, Jonny embarked on this exciting new adventure. Since then, his tremendous songwriting talents, his vocal and guitar playing skills, and his ability to connect with his audiences, have sparked a grassroots buzz that has taken his music nationwide.

Jonny's debut album, *Shades of White*, was released in August 2003 as he entered his sophomore year of college. It is a project that continues to impact thousands of lives each year. He released the follow-up CD, *Everyday God*, during his senior year of college. It has an even fuller and richer sound than *Shades of White*, yet maintains the acoustic vibe and melodic style that made his first project so popular. For his third CD, Jonny traveled to Nashville to record with producer Mitch Dane (Jars of Clay, Bebo Norman).

They Need Love released in March 2007 and immediately caught the attention of radio stations across the country thanks to his song "Hold Me," which hit the top-40 charts in 2008.

On May 5th, 2009, Jonny released his latest CD, *More Beautiful You*. This is his first as a signed artist with INO Records, the home to musicians such as MercyMe, Caedmon's Call, The Fray, and many more. This album reveals lyrics, melodies, and instrumentation that go far deeper than the stereotypical pop hit. With all the songs written or co-written by Jonny, *More Beautiful You* captivatingly illuminates Jonny's heart—a heart that is passionate about reaching his generation with the message of God's love, forgiveness, and grace.

"Instead of focusing solely on the idea of God's grace, *More Beautiful You* moves through many different aspects of the Christian faith," Jonny shares. "One theme that is prevalent throughout the record is truth. We are called to speak and live truth even in a culture that doesn't agree."

The single, "More Beautiful You," has taken the country by storm. It quickly became the most played and requested song on Christian radio. Co-penned by Jonny, the song aims to tell women they were created by God with a specific purpose in mind.

"The idea that they need to look a certain way in order to be feel beautiful is completely false," Jonny explains. "Through this song I hope to get the attention of females and tell them

the truth found in God's Word, that there could never be a more beautiful you!"

Jonny has had the opportunity to open in concert for some of Christian music's biggest acts (MercyMe, Steven Curtis Chapman, Tenth Avenue North). He has also performed at some of the largest Christian music festivals in the country. Although he primarily travels as an acoustic act, Jonny has an amazing group of musicians who join him for full-band shows.

God has taken Jonny on an incredible journey over the past few years. Joined by his wonderful wife, Libby, he is ready to follow wherever God leads.

For more information:

Go to Jonny's website at www.jonnydiaz.com

or check out his MySpace™ page at:

www.myspace.com/jonnydiaz.

Prayer of Salvation

God loves you—no matter who you are, no matter what your past. God loves you so much that He gave His one and only begotten Son for you. The Bible tells us that "...whoever believes in him shall not perish but have eternal life" (John 3:16 NIV). Jesus laid down His life and rose again so that we could spend eternity with Him in heaven and experience His absolute best on earth. If you would like to receive Jesus into your life, say the following prayer out loud and mean it from your heart.

Heavenly Father, I come to You admitting that I am a sinner. Right now, I choose to turn away from sin, and I ask You to cleanse me of all unrighteousness. I believe that Your Son, Jesus, died on the cross to take away my sins. I also believe that He rose again from the dead so that I might be forgiven of my sins and made righteous through faith in Him. I call upon the name of Jesus Christ to be the Savior and Lord of my life. Jesus, I choose to follow You and ask that You fill me with the power of the Holy Spirit. I declare that right now I am a child of God. I am free from sin and full of the righteousness of God. I am saved in Jesus' name. Amen.

If you prayed this prayer to receive Jesus Christ as your Savior for the first time, please contact us on the Web at:

www.harrisonhouse.com to receive a free book.

Or you may write to us at

Harrison House · P.O. Box 35035 · Tulsa, Oklahoma 74153